NEEDLEPOINT
STITCHERY

NEEDLEPOINT STITCHERY

MARGARET BOYLES

Macmillan Publishing Co., Inc.
New York
Collier Macmillan Publishers,
London

MACMILLAN Publishing Co., Inc.
866 Third Avenue, New York, N.Y. 10022
Collier-Macmillan Canada Ltd., Toronto, Ontario

Designed and produced in association with
Chanticleer Press, Inc., New York, and
printed at Amilcare Pizzi, S.p.A., Milan, Italy
Design: Roberta Savage

Library of Congress Catalog Card Number:
72-77274

FIRST PRINTING

Most grateful thanks are extended to all my friends at the Columbia Minerva Corporation for their friendly interest in this book and their generous contribution of all the yarns and canvas used to prepare the needlepoint illustrations. Also, fondest thanks to my editors and friends, who offered me the rewarding opportunity of writing this book.

CONTENTS

This book is dedicated lovingly to my grandmother, Margaret Kyle James, who really started it all by teaching me that it is fun to use a needle. Every little girl should have a grandmother who knows the secrets of making "monkeys" from fabric scraps.

This sampler demonstrates a variety of stitches possible on needlepoint canvas.

Detail from Geometric Pillow. *A pillow top with a design created entirely by the interplay of different stitches. The design is geometric and very effective in shades of green, red, and orange. Design is entirely dependent on the stitches and colors.*

As a traveling representative for the world's largest manufacturer of hand knitting yarns and needlework supplies, I have already met many of my readers. Women of all ages, all interests, and all economic levels have asked me many questions. It is really these women who have written this book, for their questions form its basis. It is hoped that, by putting the answers to all the questions in one volume, a reference will be created that will enable both the beginner and the more advanced needlewoman to enrich her needlepoint. Many of the sections contain information that is very basic, but there are pointers throughout that will enable even the skilled to improve their needlepoint.

One of the most exciting facets of needlepoint is that it is a mirror of our times and, like the times, it has changed. At one time most needlepoint was a dreary chore. What could be more uninspiring than working those millions of little black background stitches around a Victorian nosegay that someone else had already had the fun of working?

This is no longer true. Needlepoint is fun! Color and design in needlepoint, just as color and design in the fine arts, have changed to reflect our attitudes. Young and skilled artists are now interested in most forms of handcrafts and embroideries and are giving us good designs that are worth the time it takes to work them. The fact that these are now available is probably the reason that so many young people are busy stitching away at their needlepoint.

But it is not just the young who are interested in needlepoint. Nor is it just the women who are stitching away. Needlepoint is an age-old art, but it has never before enjoyed the popularity that it enjoys today.

Manufacturers have contributed much to the change in needlepoint. Yarns of excellent quality are available in a fantastic array of colors; good canvases, well designed kits, and a wide choice of design are available readily in small shops and large department stores in large cities and small towns alike. The only major difficulty now is deciding among the many offerings.

The "new" needlepoint is here and that is what this book is all about. The trend is toward the use of some of the lesser-known, fancy needlepoint stitches, and this book illustrates many of them as well as the more traditional stitches. In addition to the needlepoint stitches, a selection of embroidery stitches that work on needlepoint canvas has been included. Combined, these two types of stitches produce a new look in canvas embroidery which is becoming increasingly popular.

Although the use of stitches is emphasized in this book, the embroiderer's skill is still basic to good needlepoint, so every attempt has been made to cover all the technical details that make up good needlepoint. All steps, from preparing the canvas to finishing and blocking, are discussed and illustrated. There is even a section on designing and transferring your own design on the canvas. Also included is a Design Portfolio featuring a dozen ready-to-work designs created especially for this book.

Although this book covers all phases of needlepoint throughly, it is only a beginning. Hopefully it is an inspiration, for canvas embroidery developed to its fullest can become a fine art. Experiment. Have fun! The old rules are relaxed, and you can enjoy yourself. Create your own "new" needlepoint.

Margaret Boyles

1
MATERIALS

One of the happiest results of the current vogue for needlepoint is that the materials for this type of embroidery are now readily available. Supplies, which were once found only in speciality shops and boutiques, are now available everywhere. There are wide selections of yarns and canvases from which to choose. Kits offer a variety of subjects and a convenience that is not to be discounted. Beautiful hand-painted and screened designs abound; even the traditional canvas, with the pattern already worked, has been updated with contemporary colors and designs.

Needlepoint materials should be chosen with care. When yarn, canvas, and needle are perfectly matched and of fine quality, the embroidery goes smoothly and is a relaxing, soothing pastime. If only one of the elements is faulty, the problems are vexing enough to frustrate even the most skillful embroiderer. Take time to learn about the materials and then the further time necessary to find them.

CANVAS

Needlepoint is embroidery on canvas. Therefore, it is the canvas that provides the unique quality. The canvas, either of cotton or linen fibers, has an even weave of open mesh or squares. It is made in many different sizes, the number of threads or squares per inch determining the number of stitches that will be worked to the inch of canvas. The larger the number of threads to the inch, the smaller (and more numerous) the stitches will be. This thread count is the key to that often confusing list of terms used to describe the size of the needlepoint stitches. Petit point, gros point, and quick point are the names that describe the size of the stitches. Petit point stitches, worked on fine canvas or silk gauze, usually number from fourteen to a hundred stitches to the inch. Gros point stitches count from seven to fourteen to the inch. Quick point, sometimes called Ponto Grado, is a term coined to denote very large stitches varying from three to six per inch.

Needlepoint canvas is made in two very distinct types or weaves: mono, sometimes called uni or congress, canvas; and penelope, or double, canvas. Both are available in white and ecru. The color has nothing whatever to do with the quality of the canvas, but it should be considered when a project is being planned. The canvas will be less apparent if you use an ecru canvas rather than a white canvas when working with dark-colored yarns. If the stitch does not completely cover

Mono Canvas

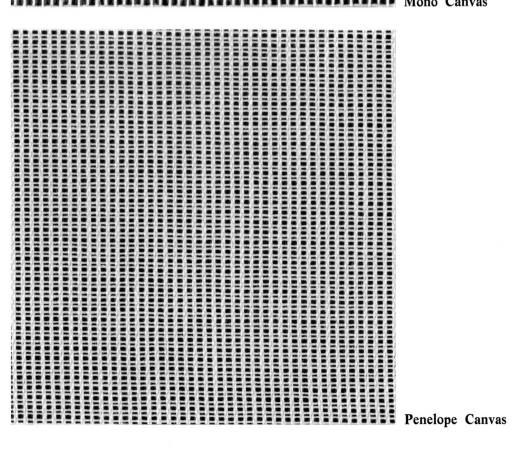

Penelope Canvas

the canvas, the contrast between stitch and canvas will not be as great. For light-colored yarns, the white canvas is preferable.

As its name indicates, mono canvas is woven so that one horizontal and one vertical thread intersect to form each mesh. This creates a weave that has a relatively large opening, making mono a very easy canvas on which to work and accounting, in part, for its wide use. Since the threads of mono canvas merely cross and do not interlock, this canvas requires a large amount of sizing to hold the threads in place. This is really not a disadvantage. The sizing will soften slightly as you work, but not enough to really matter.

Penelope, or double, canvas has a very distinctive weave. If you will examine the accompanying photographs of both types of canvas, you will note that in penelope canvas there are four threads forming each intersection. The two vertical threads are placed close to each other, while the two horizontal threads have a small space between them. The four threads interlock at each intersection, which makes this a very stable canvas.

Both types of canvas are woven in many sizes, which are designated by the number of threads, and therefore the number of needlepoint stitches, to the inch. Number 10 canvas, for example, is woven so that there will be ten needlepoint stitches to the inch.

Canvas is readily available in sizes from three to sixteen threads to the inch. Many other sizes for intricate petit point designs are manufactured, but they are difficult to find because demand is so small.

The unique weave of penelope canvas is what makes possible the use of both petit point and gros point stitches on the same piece of needlepoint. This is accomplished simply by pushing apart the threads of the canvas and working the tiny stitches over the single threads. For this reason, penelope canvas will often be designated by two numbers. For example, 10/20 penelope indicates that either 10 or 20 stitches or both may be worked per inch of canvas.

Very fine petit point—often called mille point—is often worked on silk gauze with a hundred threads to the inch. The gauze is then appliqued to a standard canvas and petit point and gros point are worked around it. Since this work is very tedious and difficult to see, only small amounts of mille point are ever found in one piece and the work is extremely expensive. The tiny stitches do allow a depth of detail

The Story of a Ship. *This beautiful large needlepoint "painting" is a good example of a kind of needlepoint that is fast becoming a lost art. The central figures are all worked in beautifully shaded petit point. All the heads, hands, and the ship are worked on fine silk gauze and appliqued to the canvas. The detailed background was worked over trammed threads as a guide to the colors. The mille point stitches in the faces are so tiny that they make the adjoining petit point look very large in comparison. Pieces like this are tomorrow's heirlooms, for very few are being produced today.*
(Photo courtesy of John Dritz, Scovill Manufacturing Company)

The Dancing Lesson. *Like the* Story of a Ship *on page 15, this petit point piece is accented by very fine mille point stitches. The beautifully lighted and detailed background was worked over a ground of long laid or tramé threads for further emphasis of the many details.*

that approximates painting and for this reason it is very effective. Silk threads are usually used for mille point and add greatly to its appeal. (See illustration, The Story of the Ship).

Needlepoint canvas is generally cotton, sometimes linen. In the best canvas each thread is itself made of six fine threads twisted together to form a smooth, even thread. Look at canvas carefully and critically before buying. The threads should be round and smooth. There should be no knots or other irregularities in the threads. A knotted thread may break when the finished needlepoint is blocked. Irregularities in the thickness of the threads do affect the evenness of the needlepoint stitches. An inferior canvas will have threads that have a flat appearance and an excessive amount of sizing.

It is confusing, but true, that there is another type of canvas called penelope which is not intended for needlepoint. Because you will not be satisfied if you should mistakenly start your needlepoint on this scrim, you should know about it. This canvas is much lighter in weight than needlepoint canvas and does not have the distinctive weave that belongs to the penelope canvas intended for needlepoint. The threads are spaced regularly instead of in horizontal and vertical pairs. This canvas is intended for use in counted cross-stitch embroidery and to facilitate counting every fifth thread is a bright blue. The blue lines will identify cross-stitch canvas for you immediately.

Needlepoint canvas does not have a right or wrong side until after the design has been applied to it. Mono canvas, having an even weave, does not have an "up and down" and can be turned in any direction as long as the stitch direction is not changed after the embroidery is begun. Penelope, on the other hand, should always be held so that the selvedges form the sides of the piece. If for some reason these selvedges have been removed, hold the canvas so that the two closely entwined threads run up and down.

When choosing canvas, keep in mind the final use of the piece of needlepoint. Remember that a smaller mesh size will accommodate more intricate shadings and design, but if your project is to be a bold geometric it may be just as effective in quicker, larger stitches. Tiny stitches are certainly very beautiful, but they should be reserved for the place where they will be most appreciated. To cover one square inch of number 10 canvas will take 100 stitches, but to cover the same area on number 14 canvas will require 196 stitches. The time difference is considerable. This should not be interpreted to mean that small stitches are to be avoided, but to indicate that, when choosing your canvas, the size of the stitches should be considered with the final product in mind. Good planning at the outset of a needlepoint project will pay high dividends in terms of time.

NEEDLES

The needle used for needlepoint is called a "Tapestry needle." It has an elongated eye, a tapered body, and a blunt point. Needles range in size from a very small 24 to a large 13. The accompanying chart shows canvas sizes with the needle size that is usually correct.

There can be no rule for the exact size needle that must be used with each size canvas. The needle should be small enough to pass through the canvas easily, but at the same time large enough to carry the yarn without wearing it unduly. Needles are very inexpensive so it is possible to have on hand an assortment of sizes and to experiment with the needle and yarn to determine the size that is best.

Number   5 canvas   13 needle
Number   6 canvas   16 needle
Number 10 canvas   18 needle
Number 12 canvas   18 or 19 needle
Number 14 canvas   20 needle

YARNS

This is the most exciting part of planning a needlepoint project. The glorious assortment of yarns available is one of the greatest joys of needlepoint. Just looking at them in the stores is enough to make your fingers itch to get busy with needle and canvas! With the array of colors presented, needlepoint becomes almost an art in which one paints with yarn and canvas instead of paint and canvas.

One of the most versatile and most widely used needlepoint yarns is Persian-type wool. The range of colors manufactured in this yarn is almost unbelievable, which probably accounts, in part, for its popularity. It is a three-ply strand that is easily separated into varying numbers of ply to suit many canvases. One-ply is sufficient for petit point; two-ply covers number 14 canvas; and three-ply covers number 10 canvas beautifully and can be used just as it comes from the skein. Because it is a long-wearing yarn, Persian-type is often used double (six-ply) for beautiful needlepoint rugs.

Persian-type yarn is sold in one-ounce skeins (about forty yards) as well as in small seven-yard skeins, which are economical when only a small amount of a shade is needed. There are many needlepoint specialty shops that will sell as little as a yard of this yarn.

Traditional tapestry yarn is an excellent long-wearing yarn created especially for working needlepoint on number 10 canvas. This yarn is generally moth proof, dye lot-matched, and light resistant—all very important features when needlepoint is intended for upholstery. Usually found in convenient forty-yard pull skeins, this yarn is also packaged in smaller seven-yard skeins primarily in the accent colors. Tapestry yarn works up smoothly with a minimum of fuzzing. Although the color range is not as wide as that found in Persian-type yarn, much has been done for this yarn as far as updating colors, so you can find the brightest contemporary colors as well as the beautiful muted shades that distinguish traditional pieces.

Time was when the use of anything but traditional tapestry yarn for needlepoint was taboo. Like everything else, needlepoint has changed with the times and there is a new freedom in the way we use all materials. A chair seat that is going to get hard wear should most certainly be worked in the hard-wearing tapestry yarns, but there the rules end. Any yarn can be used if it covers the canvas and answers logically to the use of the finished piece of needlepoint. If the exact shade needed for a pillow background is found in a hand knitting yarn, but not in tapestry yarn, why not use it! If fingering or baby yarns are used for petit point, the work is much smoother and swifter than if the traditional six-strand embroidery floss is used. A wool yarn in a medium or sport weight works up beautifully on number 14 canvas. When experimenting with the use of knitting yarns for needlepoint, keep in mind that these yarns are generally softer than those produced specifically for needlepoint. It is wise to use a shorter strand in the needle than you normally do. This will prevent excessive wearing during the working. The color and variety that these yarns will add are to be valued, but they should not be used in a situation in which their wearing qualities will be tested.

Because of the differences in the ways individuals work and the varying amounts of yarn that different stitches require, there is no really accurate table that can be made up to indicate how much yarn will be needed to complete a project. The only really accurate gauge is found by measuring the yards of yarn required to cover a square inch of canvas in the stitch that will be used. This yardage is then multiplied by the square inches in the area to be covered. After a little experience, the eye becomes so practiced that most needlepoint enthusiasts can easily judge at a glance the quantities needed. It is always better to purchase more yarn than you think you will need rather than to try matching an important color later. Colors are constantly being updated and changed by the manufacturers and may be discontinued at any time even if the color is one that seems basic. There is usually no problem using up leftover yarns. Very often they are the inspiration for a new project. There is also something very satisfying about having a store of colors ready for projects that are conceived quickly. A large supply of yarns on hand is something very common to the breed of craftsmen who love needlepoint.

If a needlepoint piece is to be of many colors, it may not be necessary to purchase all at one time. It is, however, very important that all background yarn be purchased at one time. Most of the problems with matched dye lots have been solved, but too much time is invested in needlepoint to risk having a poor match in background yarn.

SCISSORS, THIMBLE, AND FRAMES

A pair of good embroidery scissors is not a luxury. Fine scissors have smooth tapered blades that are sharp to the very tips. Keep them in a little case with the needlepoint so that there will never be a temptation to use them for other purposes that might damage or dull the blades. Those sharp tips are going to be needed if needlepoint stitches have to be ripped out later.

If you are accustomed to using a thimble for sewing or embroidery, by all means use it for needlepoint. However, if you belong to the school that considers a thimble bothersome, never mind. Personal comfort is the only issue here. Beautiful needlepoint can be made with or without a thimble.

There is also much debate about whether or not needlepoint should be worked on a frame. Most professional embroiderers and many European women do work only on a frame. The average American woman does not want to be bothered. The use of a frame eliminates the portability of the work and for this reason more than any other is considered undesirable. Also, when the needlepoint is mounted on a frame, it must be propped against a chair or table to allow the hands freedom to work. The whole frame must be turned over in order to end a strand of yarn and begin a new one. However, one does quickly adjust to this little inconvenience and it becomes easy to work with one hand above and one below the work. The canvas, laced tightly into the frame, will retain its original shape and condition.

Before making a decision about working on a frame, it is wise to try both methods. A very simple and inexpensive frame is a set of artist's stretcher frames. Four pine strips are cut and notched so that they fit easily together to make a rigid, light frame. The canvas is then tacked to the frame and worked.

There are many types of frames designed especially for needlepoint. The small ones with two roller sides are very good. The needlepoint is attached to the rollers and rolled from top and bottom to expose only the area that is to be worked. As the work progresses the completed embroidery is rolled out of the way and the next area to be worked is ready for the needle.

Attractive frames that have their own stands are beautiful. Many of these are copies of antiques still on display in some historic homes. Several of these still hold the needlepoint on which the famous lady was working when she died, adding to their historic value.

A visit to a well-stocked needlepoint department or store will help you to decide which frame, if any, is for you. Needlepoint, after all, is meant to be a happy pastime project and the materials used for it should all contribute to that end.

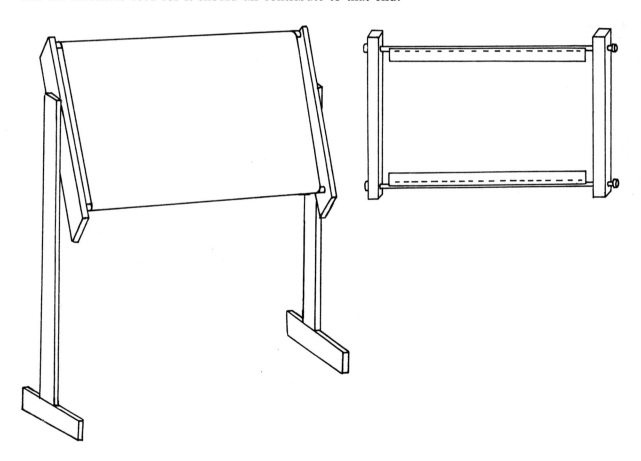

PURCHASED DESIGNS AND KITS

When you choose to begin needlepoint, there are several approaches to making the first purchase of supplies. There are kits that contain all the materials needed to complete a specific article; there is needlepoint with the design already worked for you; there are hand-painted canvases; there is plain canvas and yarn to experiment with as you please.

No matter which you choose, buy with care. A beginner's first project should be small, colorful, and useful and should contain only the best materials. To be sure that you will finish the project, buy one that you really like.

Present-day kits are fantastic. Good designers have become interested in needlepoint and the major manufacturers are putting out well-designed kits that present an ease of buying and an economy never before possible. Instructions with most kits are adequate and some are excellent. Follow the instructions carefully. The quantities of yarn in a kit are planned for the stitches given. Changing will cause problems and may cause you to run short of yarn.

Although most kits are sealed to protect the contents, do not buy one that is packaged so that you cannot see the materials it contains. Modern packaging materials make it possible to produce a package that is able to take a lot of abuse on the store counter, but can still display its contents well. You want to see what kind of canvas and yarn you are purchasing. Check also to see how much additional equipment you need to buy. Some kits will be complete even to the needle needed, while others may need to be supplemented with more yarn and/or needles.

There are many beautiful pieces of needlepoint with the center design already worked. These are available in a wide range of subjects and sizes. As a beginner project, these pieces offer an opportunity to learn the basics of needlepoint without the necessity of designing a piece.

If you have not checked these pieces recently and have visions of Victorian nosegays, check again. Much has been done for this needlepoint to update it as far as color and design go. It is now possible to find the most contemporary designs and colors as well as traditional patterns with their lovely soft colorings. A piece of this open-stock needlepoint, worked in one of the fancy background stitches, will make a very beautiful first project.

For years there were exclusive little needlepoint boutiques that sold very expensive hand-painted needlepoint. Suddenly, hand-painted needlepoint is available everywhere. Painting a canvas does have a definite advantage. If there is to be intricate shading, it is much more realistically indicated with paint than with any other medium. There is also no need to refer to a chart or diagram while working. One simply matches the yarn to the paint and stitches away.

If painted needlepoint is your choice, check the canvas to make sure that the paint has not been applied so thickly that it has clogged the holes of the canvas and will flake off as you work.

Another type of needlepoint available is that which has the design applied to it in tramé. In traméd work, the design is indicated in color with long stitches on the canvas. It is then worked over the tramé threads with matching yarn. These pieces are usually sold with a kit of yarn matched to the tramé threads.

There are also very elaborate designs charted on graph paper from which needlepoint can be worked. One starts out with a completely blank piece of canvas and, by following the chart, creates a picture with yarn. Of course, counting the squares of the design does take concentration and attention to detail, but the results are usually very lovely. Much more intricate patterns and details are possible when one works from a chart. These charts are generally imported and can be purchased in fine specialty shops.

Perhaps the happiest purchases for a beginner to make is a good book, a piece of canvas, needles, and yarn. With these you are free to experiment and learn as you please. To learn a specific stitch, you need only work a little square— two or three inches is enough. Make the little swatches in a patchwork arrangement and use it for a pillow or book cover. You may just wish to practice the stitches at random on the canvas and keep it handy with your needlepoint equipment for reference.

There is so much good needlepoint easily available that it is difficult to choose. The best possible advice is to start small and grow—grow not only in size but in scope. Begin with a simple pattern and progress to more intricate shadings and colorings as your proficiency increases. Learn some of the novelty stitches and use them in the background or the body of your designs whenever possible. Above all, have fun.

2
NEEDLEPOINT DESIGN

Even though there is much well-designed needlepoint available, there inevitably comes the moment when you want to work a piece that is of your own design. To design good needlepoint, it is not necessary that you be an accomplished artist. In fact, delightful, often whimsical, creations are produced by complete amateurs. This chapter is to help you if you are anxious to design and have no training. Don't be afraid to try. It is fun and there is no satisfaction like that of completing a piece that is your own from start to finish.

Aside from the pleasure derived from designing your own needlepoint, there is the very practical savings to be considered. The prices of custom-designed needlepoints are so high that they are almost ridiculous. Some of this "art" is also so bad that it makes most artists groan. You can have needlepoint designed just for you for the very small investment in the art supplies discussed in this chapter. No one can know better than you exactly what your needs are as far as design goes. The sources upon which you can draw are almost endless and, once you begin looking for ideas, you will soon catch yourself translating almost everything into needlepoint.

As long as you do not produce your work for sale as original art, you can copy and adapt as much as you please. Parts of one design can be combined with elements from another to create a design that fits your needs exactly.

To list here all the possible places that you will find inspiration would be valueless, since, as your eye becomes educated, you will find good ideas in seed catalogs, dress and upholstery fabrics, wallpaper, magazines, books, newspaper advertising, rugs, fashion accessories such as scarves, modern art—all sorts of media will suggest needlepoint design to you. It is a good idea to make a collection of ideas that appeal to you. You may not be ready to use an idea at the moment you find it, but it will wait for you in your scrapbook or file.

Many of today's wallpaper designs adapt well to being copied in needlepoint, for there is a trend toward brightly colored, simplified designs. It is more interesting to adapt a part of the design than it is to try to copy exactly the entire pattern. If a pattern is a floral with many kinds and shapes of flowers, take one of the more important flowers, enlarge it, and simplify it and you will have a striking emphasis for the pattern. A graphic interpretation like this will attract much more attention than a line-for-line copy ever could.

The same is true for other types of designs. For instance, to make a pillow for a room papered in a green and white cane pattern, you could enlarge the cane and change the colors to hot pink and white. A pillow that was an exact copy in color and size would blend into the background and be forgotten.

A family's interests and hobbies can inspire you to design needlepoint reflecting those interests. Nothing could be a more appreciated or personal gift than needlepoint depicting a subject that is very dear to the receiver.

There may already be a budding artist in the family and you may be treasuring some of the very appealing art that children turn out. It is easy to make a lasting memento of this art by tracing it onto canvas and embroidering it. Usually the designs are simple and boldly colored, needing no changes at all. Pieces of this type are a joy to own. In the corner, don't forget to embroider the artist's name and the date so that future generations can enjoy it also.

There are several ways that pictures in magazines can be enlarged or reduced to the size that you need. Probably the simplest and least involved is the photostatic print. Take the print to a shop that makes photostatic copies and ask to

Father-Dad Picture. *This picture makes imaginative use of both color and stitches in creating an interesting design. The stitches used are the tent stitch and the slanting Gobelin.*
(Designed by Judith Gross, photo courtesy of Columbia Minerva Corporation)

Floral Brick Cover. *These charming flowers, worked in a variety of needlepoint stitches in blues and greens, cover a brick which may be used as a door stop or as a bookend.*
(*Photo courtesy of Nina Needlepoint*)

Rooster Pillow. *This brightly colored rooster has many different stitches worked into his plummage, making him a charming example of the way the novelty stitches add to needlepoint.*
(*Photo courtesy of Nina Needlepoint*)

have the picture enlarged or reduced to the exact size that you need. The copy will not be as clear as the magazine print, but this is desirable since this will automatically eliminate some of the unwanted detail. In order to translate the picture into needlepoint, you may need to eliminate even more of the detail. Study the enlargement carefully and decide which lines are the ones that are important to the design. Go over all the lines that you want to use with a felt-tipped marker. Now it is only necessary to trace the dark lines onto the needlepoint canvas. You will find that needlepoint canvas seems almost transparent when it is laid over a design or pattern to be transferred to it. This makes transferring a design a simple task of laying the canvas over the design, lining up the design so that it is centered and straight, and drawing it on the canvas. Simply lay the canvas over the picture and trace the design onto it.

Artists make very good use of tracing paper and you will find that a pad of tracing paper is a very good investment. It is easy to work out a design right on the paper and trace it directly onto your canvas. Often, you will find that you want to combine parts of several designs into a single pattern for your needlepoint. Trace each element onto a separate piece of tracing paper. Draw the outline of the size of the needlepoint on another piece of paper. Arrange and rearrange the smaller elements within the outline until you have an arrangement that you like. Lay another piece of tracing paper over all and trace the design onto it. Go over the outline with a dark felt-tipped marker so that you can see it to trace it onto the canvas.

Simple shapes can be arranged in many ways to create interesting designs. Cut squares or circles from colored tissue paper and arrange them to overlap collage-fashion to make a pattern. Where the colors overlap there is a color change that adds interest. When the design pleases you, lay a piece of tracing paper over it and trace it.

It is usually wise to make your first design a fairly simple one as far as detail and number of colors are concerned. Progress to more complicated shadings and more intricate details in subsequent projects. Not all designs are suitable for translation into needlepoint, but one becomes familiar with, and develops a feeling for, this with experience. Sometimes a design will not look exactly like the source from which it was taken, but will have the same feeling as the original. These are the things that can only be learned by the actual experience of designing and working the needlepoint.

Whether you work from a photostat, draw your own original design, or combine elements from various designs, you will probably find a colored rendering of the design helpful. Make another tracing of the design and roughly paint or color in as you wish. This will give you a good idea of whether the placement of the colors is good. Use any medium that you can work with easily and quickly as this is for reference only. If you do not paint your canvas, you will carry this with you to work from. Also this can go shopping with you to choose yarns.

After the design has been finalized and rendered in color, it is time to prepare the canvas. Everything used on the canvas must be waterproof. This, of course, includes all markers, inks, paints, and yarns. The needlepoint will be wet for blocking and any materials that bleed into the wet yarn will ruin many hours of work. Many beautiful pieces of needlepoint have been permanently damaged when ink or paint ran into the stitches and discolored them. There is no way of repairing this damage, so it is wise to carefully check all materials before beginning to work. It takes only a few minutes to take a scrap of canvas, fasten all shades of yarn to it, mark it with the markers or paints to be used, and wet it thoroughly and leave it to dry. Any material that may cause trouble will be easy to spot and can be eliminated.

Felt-tipped markers are very good to use for transferring designs to canvas, for they are easy to handle and dry quickly. Markers must be waterproof, not just water resistant. Check the labels carefully and if you are still not certain that the pen is safe to use on your canvas, test it on a piece of canvas. Let it dry thoroughly, then soak it in water and let it dry. If it is going to bleed it will do so on the scrap.

Some of the best felt marking pens, as far as waterproofness is concerned, are unfortunately equipped with very broad tips. This problem can be overcome by shaving, with a razor blade, the felt into a tapered shape that is better for your purpose. Wide, heavy, dark lines are to be avoided, since they have a definite tendency to show through the stitches after the needlepoint has been worked.

When purchasing felt-tipped markers for use on needlepoint canvas, avoid black if possible. You will want to use the lightest possible color that will show up on the canvas. Pink and pale blue are very good. But orange and grey will also show up well enough to allow you to work comfortably.

You do not want to have to strain your eyes to see the outline, but you do want to avoid the dark shadow that will appear on your work if the lines are too dark.

Transfer a design to canvas by laying the canvas on top of the tracing and drawing in the design with a felt-tipped marking pen. It may help you to see better to do the tracing if you will lay a piece of plain white paper under the tracing paper on which the design is drawn.

To paint in the colors of the design after it has been traced onto the canvas is a personal decision. It should be noted that it is easier on the eyes to work stitches on a plain canvas than it is to work on canvas painted the exact shade as the yarn. There is also a psychological factor to be considered. Painting the design gives away what the design is going to look like when finished. If one is working on a canvas with only the outline as a guide, the design takes shape as one works. To the true needlewoman this is part of the joy of needlework. There is nothing quite like the satisfaction of seeing a design emerge as one stitches.

On the other hand, painting the canvas does have some very definite advantages. After the canvas has been painted, there is no need to refer to a chart or picture for color guidance. Intricate shadings are also more easily indicated with paint, for the canvas is treated just like a piece of art work in the painting process. A colored canvas is also very attractive and sometimes more interesting to work for this reason. Truly, one must try both a painted canvas and one that is just outlined before deciding which method is preferable.

Needlepoint canvas can be painted with either oil or acrylic paints. Oil paints are thinned with turpentine or japan thinner and applied in a very thin coat. You must be careful not to clog the canvas or put on a coat of paint thick enough to flake off during the working. An oil-painted canvas will take a long time to dry, so even though you are getting anxious to start work, be sure that you do allow plenty of drying time. Even though the canvas may feel dry to the touch, the paint in the spaces where the canvas threads join can still be damp enough to rub off on the yarn as you stitch.

The convenient new acrylic paints which are thinned with water are quicker to dry and are very good for use on needlepoint canvas. Check the manufacturer's directions for use and to make sure that they are waterproof after drying. As with the oil paints, apply a very thin coat of paint. A well-

Anne King Sampler. *This needlepoint sampler, typical of the times in which it was made, was worked by a little girl named Anne King in 1769. The flowering polychrome plant, the border chain of small abstract forms, and the lettering are worked in shades of green, blue, light brown, rose, pink, buff, and yellow on a dark brown and black background.*
(Photo courtesy of the Henry Francis du Pont Winterthur Museum)

painted needlepoint canvas has only a very small amount of color showing on the wrong side. If you turn over a canvas and find the colors almost as bright on the back as the front, you will know that too much paint has been applied.

If you are just beginning to design your own needlepoint and do not have a full complement of artist's supplies on hand, there are small starter sets available in both types of paints. If you prefer not to purchase these kits, remember that you do not need paint of every color. Usually, red, yellow, blue, black, and white are enough to mix any shades that you will need. When mixing colors you do not have to duplicate the exact shades of yarn since you are using the paint as a guide rather than as a finished work of art. As a matter of fact, it is a little bit easier to do the needlepoint if the yarn and paint are not exactly the same shade. Try, however, to make your paints slightly lighter in hue than the yarns so that the darker paints under the stitches will not darken the yarn colors.

There are some designs that you might wish to translate into needlepoint that are absolutely symmetrical or depend on intricate detailing to create the pattern. These types of designs are usually handled best if plotted first on graph paper. The stitches are then counted directly onto the canvas. This method of working does require a much larger measure of concentration, but is very rewarding and absorbing. Sometimes that great expanse of bare canvas looks very frightening, but don't be intimidated. Find the center of the graph and the center of the canvas. You can do this by folding each piece in half lengthwise, then in half crosswise. The place where the fold lines intersect is the center. Make that first stitch in the color indicated on the graph and work outward from that point.

Shifting the eyes from the needlepoint sometimes makes it difficult to keep one's place. You can lay a plain piece of paper on your graph so that the straight edge lies along the row on which you are working. This serves to draw the eye immediately to that row instead of wasting a few seconds hunting for your place. Also helpful is a gadget shaped like a clear ruler with clips on the ends so that it can be fastened right over the row being worked and will stay securely in place. The center portion of the "ruler" magnifies the row also which is very helpful.

You will find that working from a graph and counting the stitches occupies your mind completely and the hours pass

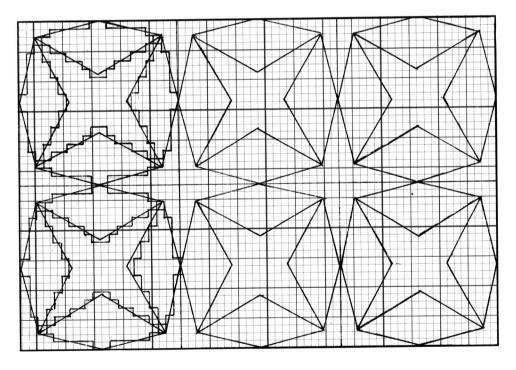

Graphing a Geometric Design. *Here a design is traced onto graph paper and necessary stitch adjustments are indicated.*

quickly and pleasantly. Seeing the design grow on the plain, unmarked canvas is stimulating and keeps one working steadily just to see how it will look after the next few stitches are worked.

Professional needlepoint designers usually prefer to do their designing on graph paper. The design is drawn onto the graph paper without regard for the little squares. After the design is satisfactory, it is blocked in following the graph paper squares as closely as possible. This method reveals exactly what the needlepoint will look like when finished, and can be a very helpful tool for the amateur designer. There are, for instance, no true curves in needlepoint, only the illusions that create a curve for the eye. When the design is placed on graph paper, any adjustments that may be necessary to make the curve more accurate are easy to see.

If you wish to place your design on graph paper to see what it will look like, prepare the drawing to the size that your finished needlepoint will be. Use graph paper with the same number of squares per inch as the canvas will have threads per inch. With pencil, trace the design onto the graph paper just as if the squares were not there. Staying as close to the outline of the tracing as possible, and using a pen, block in the design. When the ink is dry, erase the pencil lines. The result will look like finished needlepoint and will help you to see any changes that you want to make before you begin the needlepoint.

Although designing your own needlepoint may mean a small investment in artist's supplies and a venture into the world of art that you have never before considered, it is probably one of the most rewarding undertakings that you can make if you plan to do much needlepoint. The savings in money alone is enough to make the project worthwhile. This saving, however, is small compared to the enjoyment that you will reap from designing and completing a piece of needlepoint that is entirely yours from start to finish.

If you are going to design, you can have exactly what you like best to do. Some of us can spend hours happily stitching away on a background enjoying the rhythm of the stitches and the pleasant relaxation of not having to think about what we are doing. Some of us love very tiny details that require intense concentration and prevent us from thinking about anything but the stitches. Others of us like to see design and color grow and are so fond of working these areas that we fill whole canvases with masses of pattern that leave very little background to be finished. Still others of us love it all and have several projects going simultaneously, each one satisfying one of those particular needs.

If you find that your fault is not liking to work backgrounds, design so that there is a minimum of it to be done. Work all the design and begin another piece. Keep the piece requiring background to do while you are doing other things —waiting for a dentist's appointment, chatting with friends, taking a trip, sunning at the pool. If a few rows are done at a time, it is not a chore. Think positively about background work. It is a challenge to make every stitch perfect. The easy, relaxed feeling that one derives from the repetitious background stitches is part of the lure of needlepoint. The fact that needlepoint can be carried everywhere and enjoyed is one of the things that makes needlepoint so popular.

One more bit of advice to those who hate to work backgrounds. Try one or several of the novelty needlepoint stitches for your background. You will be pleasantly surprised to find that many of them work up more quickly than the tent stitch and that all of them are more interesting to do. You may find yourself looking forward to the background instead of avoiding it. Remember that you are the designer. It is up to you to make it interesting or dull.

3
THE WAY TO GOOD NEEDLEPOINT

Good needlepoint begins with good planning. A great idea may come on the spur of the moment, but it is developed into a worthwhile piece of needlepoint only with careful thought. Although thoughtful planning takes a little time, it more than makes it up in time and effort saved and in the beauty of the finished needlepoint.

Know in advance what the piece will be used for and plan size, color, pattern, and stitches with this in mind. Measure carefully since needlepoint which has been properly blocked does not shrink; nor can it be enlarged by stretching. This actually simplifies the job of measuring, for one can find the exact size needed with no guesswork involved.

Since the seams of a pillow are sewn on the last row of needlepoint stitches, the measurements are those of the desired finished size of the pillow. Small items that are constructed by sewing are also sewn on the last row of stitches. This eliminates the extra thickness in the seams that the yarn would create. If the edges look like they might fray, a line of white glue can be applied to them after they are trimmed.

If the projected piece is a chair seat, measure the upholstered portion from wood to wood at the widest points. Add one inch on both ends to allow for new padding if necessary and to give a good turn under. Make as many measurements as needed to get the correct shape. Sometimes when the chair has an irregular shape, a muslin pattern is helpful. Pin the muslin in place and mark for cutting with a pencil. Remove from chair, cut to general shape. Fit on chair again and make any necessary adjustments. Use the muslin piece as a guide to trace the outline onto the canvas.

If you have no experience with upholstery, but want to make needlepoint to upholster a large chair or sofa, it would be wise to ask a professional to cut a muslin pattern for you. The charge for this is very nominal, but could save you many hours of work. On a project of this size, all guesswork should be avoided.

After you have determined the size needed in the finished needlepoint, draw the shape on the canvas, allowing a two-inch border of canvas that will not be worked on all four sides. Some very small items may require only a one and one-half-inch border, but do not work closer than this to the edges. This canvas is not wasted. It is used for blocking and to help keep the needlepoint in shape while working.

Tape the cut edges of the canvas either with masking tape or folded bias binding. Completely enclosing the edge thus

The Author's Gold Bargello Chair. *Covered entirely in Bargello—even the sides and back of the chair—this chair was an ambitious project, but certainly rewarding when finished. Included with the needlepoint for the Bargello chapter is a swatch of the actual needlepoint and a description of the colors and pattern (page 132).*

prevents the yarn from becoming entangled with the stiff threads as you work. The tape will also prevent the edges from fraying.

If you are making a very irregularly shaped piece of needlepoint, draw the outline on the canvas and work only that portion, but keep the canvas either rectangular or square in shape until after it has been blocked.

Sometimes there is just too much extra canvas in the borders of the piece, making it unwieldy and hard to handle. It is all right to trim the edges in this case, but be sure to retain two inches of border on all sides.

THREADING THE NEEDLE

Shown on the accompanying drawings are two methods of threading a needle with yarn. There is also another very simple method that is entirely correct to use that is seldomly used. Simply press the end of the yarn tightly between the thumb and forefinger of the left hand. With the right hand force the eye of the needle between the tightly held fingers where the yarn is held. The yarn will fit right into the needle. This method works well after only a little practice. No matter what method you use, never wet or twist the yarn to insert it into the needle.

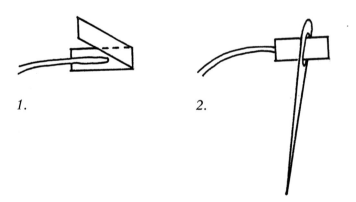

1.   2.

The Paper Method of Threading a Needle

1. *Cut a small piece of paper narrow enough to pass through the eye of the needle and about an inch long. Fold the paper as shown in the drawing and place the cut end of the yarn in the fold.*
2. *Pass folded end of the paper through the eye of the needle and the yarn will be carried through easily.*

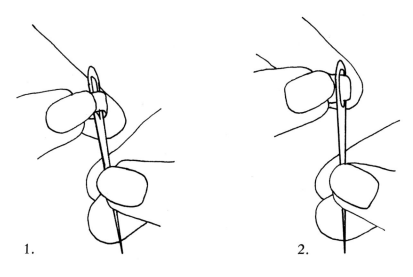

1.   2.

Threading the Needle

1. *Hold the needle between the thumb and forefinger of your right hand with the eye of the needle facing you. Fold the yarn across the needle and pull it tightly to form a fold. Hold the fold tightly with the left hand and withdraw the needle gently.*

2. *Force fold through the eye of the needle.*

The length of the strand of yarn in the needle is very important. Yarn wears thin if it is carried in and out of the canvas an excessively long time. Conversely, too many short ends on the wrong side are not desirable. Generally speaking, the finer the canvas, the shorter the yarn should be. A good length for number 10 canvas is eighteen inches. For petit point, eight to ten inches is sufficient. Large-mesh rug canvas, however, "eats" the yarn very quickly, so a longer strand can be used.

The needle should be in a position about three inches from the end of the strand of yarn. Three inches is enough to securely anchor the needle so that it will not slip off the yarn, but makes carrying a double strand of yarn through the canvas necessary for only a short time. This saves wear on the end of the yarn and allows you to work closer to the end than if you wore the yarn thin.

Yarn, needle, and canvas must fit together perfectly to insure easy stitching. The needle must be large enough to carry the yarn, but not so large that it forces the threads of the canvas apart. The yarn must be lofty enough to cover the canvas threads completely, but not so heavy that it causes a strain on the canvas. A canvas worked with yarn that is too heavy will be stiff and hard. Too heavy a yarn will also cause the stitches to look blurred and fuzzy.

STITCHING THE CANVAS

For those who have never tried needlepoint, the blank canvas is an immediate problem. How does one attach the yarn to begin the first row? The easiest method is to bring the needle up from the back, leaving about a half-inch end of yarn on the back. Begin to stitch, holding the loose end on the back with the index finger of the left hand. Stitch over and through the loose end. After about four stitches, the end is fastened.

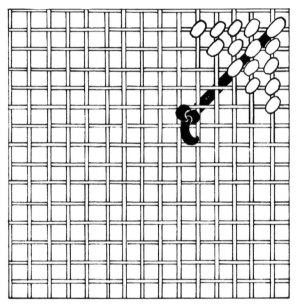

Waste Knot

The only knot ever used in needlepoint is the waste knot shown in the drawing. It is called a waste knot because it is placed on the right side of the canvas and cut away after the end has been secured.

To make a waste knot, make a knot in the end of the yarn. Go down into the canvas about six mesh from the space into which the first stitch is to be placed. Come up in the space for the first stitch. Using whichever stitch you have elected to use, begin to stitch, working over and catching the yarn until you have reached the knot. Cut away the knot and the remaining little end will fall through to the wrong side.

If one length of yarn is not long enough to complete the first row, work until the end of yarn is about two inches long. Complete a stitch by taking the needle to the wrong side. Unthread the needle and let the yarn hang free. Fasten a new thread by pulling it through the last four stitches worked. Continue working across the row for several inches, taking care not to catch the loose end in your work. Go back and thread the loose end into the needle and pull it through the first four stitches worked with the second strand.

On all successive rows the ends of yarn are fastened by pulling them through a few stitches of the previous row. When ending a strand of yarn, always be careful to go forward in the direction in which you were working. Changing the direction in which the yarn is pulled changes very slightly the shape of the stitch and affects the evenness of the overall appearance of the needlepoint.

It would be almost impossible to have the wrong side of the needlepoint as perfect as the right side, but it should be kept neat. Clip short the ends of strands of yarn. Long ends left dangling on the wrong side tangle and are often pulled through to the right side with successive stitches. This problem can be very annoying when a lot of colors are being used.

As one works, the yarn twists in the needle and does not cover the canvas well. Do not try to continue to work with the twisted yarn. Lift the canvas and let the needle hang free. It will quickly unwind itself and be ready to use again.

It is possible to prevent the yarn from twisting while working. As the needle is drawn out of the canvas at the completion of a stitch, roll it about one-quarter turn in the direction of the canvas. A little pressure from the thumb is all it takes to do this and it quickly becomes automatic. This may be surprisingly simple, but it really works.

The question of where to start working on a needlepoint canvas is one that must be answered by studying the canvas itself. Different canvases will require different approaches. The following discussion solves some of the commoner problems, but it cannot answer for every canvas. The best basic rule is to make working the easiest it can possibly be.

If your canvas is one on which a central design has already been worked, the beginning point will be determined by your choice of stitches. The continental and basket weave stitches start in the upper right corner. The horizontal half cross-stitch begins in the upper left corner. The vertical half cross and diagonal stitches start in the lower right corner. For further information, see chapter 5.

If you will be working the design yourself, it is usually best to begin work with the design area, near the center of the canvas, and work outward to the edges. However, each piece must be examined separately. If the design is a small central one, it would certainly be wiser to complete the design and treat the background like one of the above purchased with the design already worked.

Very large pieces which are to be worked completely and are not to be worked on a frame, are usually best worked outward from the center. The canvas is not as bulky in the hand before it is worked so this method keeps the size of the roll in the hand at a minimum.

Each person develops her own tension as she works. It is desirable that the needlepoint stitches be worked with a tension that is light enough to allow the yarn to cover the canvas well, but is, at the same time, firm and even. Stitches that are too tight cause undue stress on the canvas threads and make blocking difficult if not impossible.

As one works, the rhythm of the stitches becomes automatic and the tension is adjusted naturally. It should not take much concentration to make even, neat stitches, since this is something that will come with practice. Don't expect it to happen in the first row, but it will not be long before you are making perfect stitches without even thinking about them.

The stitches that are worked upright on the canvas—brick, upright Gobelin, bargello, etc.—should be worked with a slightly looser tension. This allows the yarn to lie better and cover the canvas more completely.

To make working easier, the canvas should be rolled while it is worked. Roll it up from the bottom to a point a few inches from the area to be worked first. Pin the roll on each side with a large safety pin. As the top section of the needlepoint is worked, roll it downward and pin it also. This keeps the finished embroidery clean and out of the way, and makes the canvas easy to handle.

When you put your canvas away between embroidery sessions, roll it in a clean towel, or roll it and place it in a plastic bag. Folding the canvas is not good for it. The constant folding and refolding along the same line of the canvas will break the sizing and may eventually weaken the threads in that area.

A handsome bag in which to keep your needlepoint supplies is a wise investment. One of the joys of needlepoint is that it is portable and can travel with you. Keep all your supplies

in the bag, ready to go. Remember to keep those sharp little embroidery scissors in their own case inside the bag so that there is no chance that they damage your needlepoint.

When you have a canvas on which you have a design already worked in petit point and you wish to work the back-

The Correct Method of Working a Gros Point Background around a Petit Point Design.
(Photo courtesy of the Columbia Minerva Corporation)

ground in gros point, work the gros point in as close to the petit point as possible. You will see that there are some single threads on the edge of the design on which the gros point stitch simply will not fit. The ply of the yarn is divided and these small stitches are worked in continental stitch to fit around the design. In some of the areas near the edges of the design, you will want to use the gros point stitches, but some of the very tiny areas will look better completely filled in with petit point. The photograph is an enlargement of part of a large piece showing the proper way to combine the two sizes of stitches. Note that the larger gros point stitches emphasize the smallness of the petit point and accent its beauty.

CORRECTING MISTAKES

A good needleworker is always a good ripper. It is a mistake to leave a flaw in your work. It will always be very obvious to you, even if no one else seems to notice. Ripping may be tedious, dull work, but it is always worthwhile if it results in an improvement.

If only a stitch or a few stitches need be removed, carefully snip the stitch. With the tip of the needle, carefully rip out the stitches on either side of the cut until the yarn is long enough to be threaded into the needle. Fasten off the two ends of yarn on the wrong side as you would any other end. With a new piece of yarn, rework the spaces where the stitches were removed.

When a large area is to be ripped, it is better to rip the stitches, one by one, with the tip of the needle than to risk cutting the canvas by cutting out whole rows of stitches. A cut canvas is permanently damaged and weakened. Keep the yarn cut short as you rip so that you do not have a long end to pull through with each stitch. This will allow you to rip faster. The yarn should not be reused anyway, so the clipping is not wasteful.

Use a little psychology when a large area needs to be ripped out and the work will not seem as tedious. Alternate a few minutes of ripping with a few minutes of working in a different area. If a little bit is ripped between each needleful of yarn, the job is soon done.

If you should accidentally cut a thread of your canvas or find a weak one, it is possible to strengthen that spot. Take a thread from the edge of the canvas and weave it in and out, duplicating the weave as closely as possible. Extend the thread five or six mesh beyond the cut on either side. Work over the threads and you will have an invisible mend.

Larger damage may be mended by using a patch of matching canvas. Cut a patch about one-half inch larger than the damaged area. Baste it to the wrong side of the canvas, matching the weave carefully. Work over the double thickness.

PIECING CANVAS

Although it is not desirable, it is possible to piece a needlepoint canvas. The canvas to be added must be identical to the one that is to be enlarged. Matching the weave, overlap the two for a distance of about one-half inch. Baste firmly in place. Work through the two thicknesses as if they were one. Since the canvas is so much thicker in this area, it will probably be necessary to work each stitch in two motions rather than one to cover the double thickness. That is the only difficulty that you will encounter. The extension will be strong and, if worked in the same tension as the rest of the piece, should be invisible.

4
THOUGHTS ABOUT USING THE STITCHES

Any needlepoint design can be stitched simply and adequately by using a combination of the basic slanting tent stitches. But, the use of decorative stitches within a piece can make all the difference in the world between a piece that is merely competent and one that is really exciting and which invites enthusiastic compliments from all who see it. Take for example, the tropical birds shown in the photograph—one of the exclusive designs from the Design Portfolio.

Although both birds are worked in exactly the same colors, one bird is worked in many stitches and the other is entirely in the tent stitch. Both are beautiful pieces of needlepoint. However, the bird which uses more stitches has a much livelier look and required one-fourth as many hours to work. Using the leaf stitch as a background suggests a leafy bower without actually drawing in the separate leaves. The addition of just this background would do much for the tent stitch bird. Also, the shading and the curves of the body and tail are more easily carried out with the embroidery stitches.

This book presents and illustrates many stitches—both traditional needlepoint stitches and regular embroidery stitches—that can be used creatively for canvas embroidery. These are by no means all the stitches, or stitch variations, that can be suitable for this work, but they represent a collection of those most practical and attractive. Utilizing these stitches can add much pleasure to needlepoint embroidery, for the way an individual uses the stitches becomes as personal as a signature.

When an original design is first visualized, it has color and form as well as texture. The texture will immediately suggest a certain stitch, or combination of stitches, to the needlewoman who is already familiar with the array of needlepoint stitches which can be used. For this reason, it is practical to experiment with the stitches on a piece of canvas to be kept in your work basket for reference. To become adept at a stitch, you need only work a small sample: usually a two-inch square is adequate. If you wish, you can even work the squares patchwork fashion and use the sample piece as a pillow top or book jacket. A long narrow piece can be a bell pull. There are many ways to use the sampler if you do not wish to keep it just as a reference. No matter how you choose to use the sampler, do make one to learn some of the stitches and develop a feeling for how they can be used most effectively.

With so many stitches at hand, it may be tempting at first to use as many as possible in one piece. Although it is pos-

Pair of Tropical Birds. *This pair of pictures illustrates graphically the difference that can be made in a needlepoint piece by utilizing some of the novelty stitches as well as some of the embroidery stitches.*

Practice Sampler. *Worked in wool and silk on cotton canvas, this mid-nineteenth-century sampler was probably a record of motifs for application on other pieces as needed. Many samplers of this type are found in museums, indicating that this was the common way of keeping a record of patterns. This one is especially attractive since the lady who made it had a great sense of color.*
(Photo courtesy of the Smithsonian Institution)

sible to use a large variety of stitches on a single piece of needlepoint, it is best to avoid using stitches "for stitches' sake." This approach can have a ludicrous if not unattractive result. Each stitch should be carefully chosen as part of an overall design. The stitches adapt themselves best to definite circumstances and their proper use adds to their attractiveness.

As one works with the stitches, it becomes obvious that large square-shaped stitches will not adapt to small rounded areas. They won't fit to begin with, and will make a circle look ragged rather than rounded. Often, where a Scotch stitch will not fit, mosaic, its smaller relative, will be perfect. When a large patterned stitch is good in one area, but will not fit into smaller detailed portions of a design, taper the larger stitches gradually into the tent stitch as in the face and feet of the dragon on page 118 in the Design Portfolio.

Some stitches create definite horizontal or vertical lines. Play this to its best advantage where this effect is needed, but avoid it if the directional lines will interfere with the basic design. Other stitches are definitely raised naturally and are used when part of the design is to be lifted out of the background and thus emphasized. These same raised stitches, scattered over a background of a wall hanging, will reflect light and give definite shadings. Many different stitches combined thus can be very dramatic.

Because of their very nature, the embroidery stitches allow much more freedom than the needlepoint stitches and combine with the needlepoint to fabricate canvas embroidery with a fresh, light-hearted feeling not possible otherwise.

The stitches in the book will be just as valuable to the reader who purchases her designs ready-made as to the one who designs her own, for there are many ways to use the stitches on canvases available in the stores. Since most of the stitches work best on mono canvas, look for this type of canvas. Purchase your yarn and try some of the stitches in the way that you think they will be most effective. You may begin by using just one of the stitches to work the background, but if you do even this much you are on your way. There is no way to learn to appreciate the stitches except by using them and, once you try, you realize how much you have been missing.

If you have purchased your needlepoint packaged as a kit, you are limited to exactly the colors and stitches that the manufacturer suggests and it is important that the directions are followed explicitly, for he usually guarantees that there

are sufficient quantities in the kit to finish it if this is done. However, if you find exactly what you are looking for in a kit, and you are willing to take a chance, you can find out if there is enough yarn in the kit to change stitches. With scrap yarn that has been cut into 18-inch lengths, work one square inch using the manufacturer's suggested stitch and stitching method. Keep track of the amount of yarn used. Then work one square inch of the stitch that you wish to substitute. If the new stitch takes no more yarn than the suggested one, you are safe in switching stitches. This method

A Cat. *Worked by a young girl at the Bromley Grammar School in Great Britain, this colorful cat is cleverly utilizing a great many needlepoint stitches. Even the background is full of different textures and colors which add to its charm. (Photo courtesy of B. T. Batsford Ltd.)*

is reliable if you are careful in your calculations, but remember that since you have not followed instructions, you cannot hold the manufacturer responsible. Therefore, it is better to find your design without yarn and to proceed from there.

The methods and ways that one uses the stitches of needlepoint are not the most important factors. Most important is the fact that the stitches are discovered and used. Experiment with them and you will be surprised how easily you can master them.

5
THE
BASIC
STITCH

Whenever needlepoint is mentioned, what comes to mind immediately are straight rows of small slanting stitches marching neatly across a canvas. The stitch is oval in shape and always slants upward from lower left to upper right and fits so closely to its neighbors that it completely covers the canvas to create the prized fabric which is needlepoint.

The stitch is so widely used that many do not realize that there are more than two hundred different stitches that can be used in needlepoint. This stitch's versatility and practicality, as well as its universal acceptance, have combined to make it needlepoint's basic stitch. Used alone it forms a beautiful long-wearing fabric; combined with other stitches, it accents their showy textures.

What is not always known is that there are four completely different stitching techniques that produce this basic stitch: the half cross-stitch, the continental stitch, the basket weave stitch and the diagonal stitch. They are usually referred to collectively as the tent stitch because on the surface, all look very much alike—smooth even stitches slanting upward across one intersection of the canvas. To see the differences in the stitches one must examine the wrong sides.

When the continental stitch is used, a long diagonal thread connects the stitches on the wrong side. The wrong side of the basket weave stitch reveals the source of its name. Working the stitch creates an intriguing woven pattern on the back. The back of the diagonal stitch shows a pattern of small split stitches that look very much as if they had been knitted. A close look at the wrong side of the half cross-stitch shows the small amount of yarn that is placed on the wrong side of the work by this stitch.

The Basic Needlepoint Stitch. *The half cross, continental, basket weave and diagonal stitches all produce a surface similar to this. Hence, the collective title of Tent Stitch.*

Wrong Side of Continental Stitch

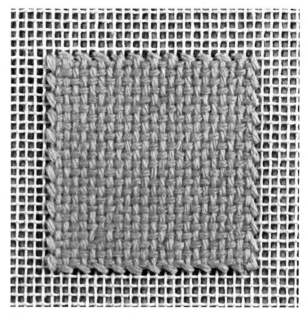

Wrong Side of Basket Weave Stitch

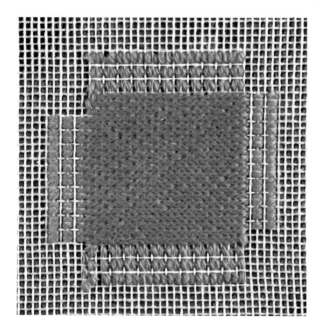

Wrong Side of Diagonal Stitch

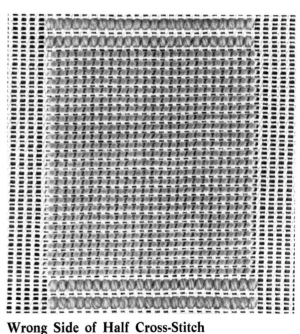

Wrong Side of Half Cross-Stitch

New England Chair Seat. *This beautiful chair seat was worked entirely in the tent stitch in wool on linen canvas. It came from New England and is dated 1750.*
(*Photo courtesy of the Smithsonian Institution*)

Following are detailed discussions of each of the tent stitches. As noted and discussed with each stitch, each of these stitches has certain advantages and disadvantages. The final purpose of the finished needlepoint should be the determining factor when you decide which one should be used for a specific piece of needlepoint. For this reason, the beginner should master all four stitches at the outset of her venture into needlepoint. All are useful and all have their correct usage.

The stitch charts are clear and easy to follow. Since all stitches except the half cross-stitch work well on mono canvas, all are drawn on mono. If you are working on penelope canvas, consider the double threads as one thread and follow the charts accordingly.

To those who have never been successful in teaching themselves stitches from a chart, I would like to say that I believe that, if you really want to, you can learn from these diagrams. Follow the instructions carefully. Read one sentence and do what it tells you to do before proceeding to the next one. Take your time and relax with the instructions. Before you know it you will be stitching away even if you have never before attempted needlepoint. Read the following stitch instructions with canvas, yarn, needle, and scissors at hand, for this is a working book and you will want to try the stitches rather than just read about them.

THE HALF CROSS-STITCH

The simplest of the needlepoint stitches is the half cross-stitch. It is exactly what its name indicates—one-half of a cross-stitch. There are two methods of working the half cross. One is worked in rows vertically up the canvas from the lower right corner. The other is worked in horizontal rows across the canvas from the upper left corner. The two working methods require the same amount of yarn and produce very similar results.

The half cross-stitch is not as popular with most needle-pointers as are the continental and basket weave stitches, but it should be mastered for it does have definite advantages. In situations where a less thick fabric is needed—such as for pictures, pillows, or very small items that become hard to finish if they are too thick—the half cross-stitch is very useful. When the amount of yarn to be used is to be kept at a minimum, the half cross-stitch again is good, for it uses one-fourth less yarn than either the basket weave or continental stitches. Many feel that the half cross does not cover the canvas as well as it should. It will cover if worked with a slightly looser tension.

Although it is not as frequently used as the horizontal half cross-stitch, the vertically worked stitches are plumper and more regular than those obtained by working horizontally. The stitch is also faster when worked vertically, since it is never necessary to work a return row bringing up the needle in the spaces of the first row, which would make it possible to split the stitches of the first row.

The vertical, or simplified, half cross-stitch

To work the vertical half cross-stitch, anchor the yarn using one of the methods described in Chapter 3, so that you will be ready to make your first stitch in the lower right corner of the canvas. The row is worked upward from the bottom to the top. The yarn is ended and the second row begun again at the bottom in the space immediately to te left of the first stitch.

The Fishing Lady. *This was a popular subject at the time it was worked (probably in Boston, Massachusetts, in the mid-1700s). Worked in the tent stitch on fine canvas with crewel yarns, the scene is very colorful and abounds with activity. The colors are realistic and the shading is very accurate.*
(Photo courtesy of the Henry Francis du Pont Winterthur Museum)

Muskrat Pillow. *This unlikely subject for a needlepoint pillow has, nonetheless, been worked into a very handsome design. It was worked entirely in the tent stitch.*
(Photo courtesy of Nina Needlepoint)

American Chair Seat and Detail. *This beautiful petit point piece was apparently intended as a chair seat, but it could just as easily have been a cushion top or a screen panel. Worked entirely in silk in the tent stitch, the piece is probably American, circa 1740.*
(Photo courtesy of the Smithsonian Institute)

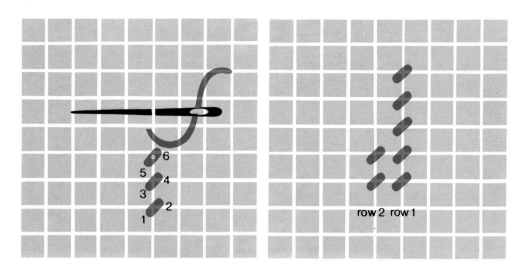

Vertical Half Cross-stitch

Following the chart, bring the needle up in the space numbered 1. Go down at 2 diagonally across one intersection of the canvas. Bring the needle up at 3, which is directly above 1. When you go down at 4, you will see that you can insert the needle straight under the bar and come up in the same motion at 5. This makes the stitching faster and easier. Continue in this manner to the top of the row.

The horizontal half cross-stitch

The horizontal half cross-stitch is worked in horizontal rows across the canvas beginning in the upper left corner. Anchor the yarn using one of the methods described in Chapter 3. Bring the needle up at 1 in the space for the first stitch. Go down at 2 diagonally across the first intersection. Slide the needle under the bar and come up at 3 immediately to the right of 1. Continue in this manner to the end of the row.

Horizontal Half Cross-stich

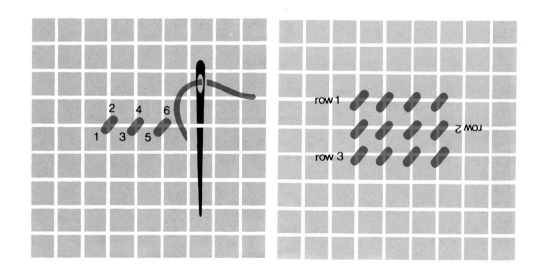

At the end of the row the canvas can be turned completely around and the return row worked, or the yarn can be ended and the second row begun again at the right side. Either method is entirely correct. It is usually faster to begin the new row at the left side. This method eliminates the necessity of bringing up the needle in a way that can split the stitches of the first row.

THE CONTINENTAL STITCH

The long, diagonal threads formed on the back of the canvas by this stitch create a natural padding of yarn that adds greatly to the durability of needlepoint worked in this stitch. This makes the continental a favorite for upholstery. Although the continental stitch does have a tendency to pull the canvas out of shape, needlepoint worked in this stitch can usually be straightened successfully by blocking. For this reason, those who favor this stitch for its very smooth texture and excellent coverage of the canvas tend to ignore the distortion.

Continental Stitch

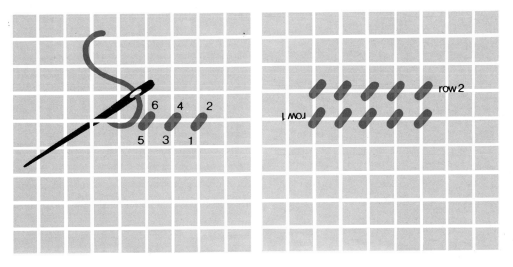

The continental stitch is very maneuverable and adapts well to working small design areas in which the basket weave becomes impractical or, to many, impossible. Many times when a design area is to be worked in basket weave—the needlepointer's choice entirely—she will first outline the area with the continental stitch since it is so much easier to handle. The continental stitch is worked in horizontal rows across the canvas from the upper right corner. Again it is proper to work across the canvas, turn the piece completely around and work the return row back, or you may end the yarn at the end of the row and start the next row again at the right side.

The faster way is to end every row at the left side of the piece and begin again at the right side.

The continental stitch begins easily by bringing the needle up at 1 in the space for the first stitch. Use any of the methods of anchoring the yarn described in Chapter 3, but the simplest method is just to hold the little end with your index finger of the left hand and work through it. Go down at 2 diagonally across the first intersection of the canvas and in the same motion slide the needle under two bars and come up at 3, which is immediately to the left of 1. Following the chart, continue across the row. If your row of stitches has an uneven appearance, it is probably because your tension is uneven. Try to pull each stitch to the same shape. It will take a little practice in the beginning, but soon you will accomplish this with no thought at all. Be careful not to pull too tightly. Stitches that are too tight prevent the needlepoint from being blocked straight when it is finished. Also, stitches put in too tightly will not cover the canvas properly.

THE BASKET WEAVE STITCH

The basket weave stitch is worked in diagonal rows beginning in the top right corner of the canvas. Although it is a little harder to master than the continental stitch, the basket weave is very interesting to work and many people believe that it is the only proper stitch to use because they are so intrigued with it. The needlepoint fabric created by the basket weave is well padded and suitable for upholstery since it wears well. The stitch has a definite advantage in that it does not distort the canvas, nor does it put any strain on the threads of the canvas. These are definite advantages.

The basket weave stitch is easy to master once it is understood that each row is one stitch longer than the previous row. The trick in working this stitch is to remember that the first stitch of the row that is upward is placed directly under the last stitch of the last row. The first stitch of the row that is worked downward is placed on the same row, but one mesh to the left of the final stitch of the previous row. These are the two key stitches that maintain the straight edges.

Begin the basket weave by fastening the yarn end using one of the methods described in Chapter 3. Bring the needle up at 1 in the space for the first stitch. Go down at 2 across one intersection of the canvas and in the same motion, pass the needle under two bars to come up at 3, one bar to the

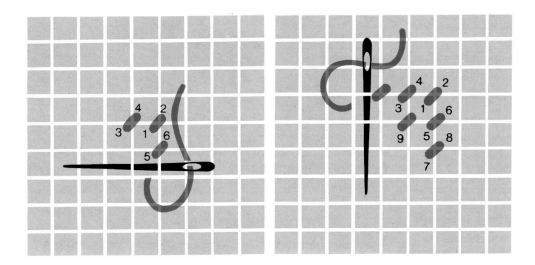

left of 1. When you go down at 4 pass the needle under two horizontal bars to come up at 5. When you go down at 6 you will have completed row two, which is only two stitches long. Notice in the drawing that the needle is in position to make the stitch formed by coming up at 7 and going down into the canvas at 8. Row three will be worked upward following the diagram to complete row three, which is three stitches long.

The needle is shown in the two diagrams for the basket weave stitch to bring attention to the fact that, when working downward, the needle is always in a vertical position; when working upward, the needle is always parallel to the horizontal threads of the canvas.

Many people enjoy working the basket weave stitch, but, unfortunately, very few do it correctly.

The fact that it is so often poorly worked does not mean that the basket weave stitch should be avoided. To the contrary, it is an excellent stitch with a beautifully textured surface. It is often said that the test of a good needlepointer is whether she can work out intricate little design sections in this stitch. Once mastered, it is one of the most interesting stitches to do and certainly a very practical stitch to use for many purposes. There are several pitfalls that can be easily avoided. The most important thing to remember is that one row is worked upward and the next row is worked on the downward slant. It is most important that this sequence be maintained to avoid the ugly diagonal lines that so often mar otherwise beautiful work. In the beginning it is fairly easy for a beginner to lose her place and forget in which direction she was working. Try never to end a strand of yarn at the exact end of a row without first beginning a new piece and working just a few stitches. The back of the stitches will also tell you in which way you were working. Make a few stitches. If the pattern weave does not match, you will know that you have started out in the wrong direction. An accomplished needlepointer can tell at a glance the direction of her last row simply by looking at the back of the work, but this takes a little experience.

The ends of the strands of yarn used for basket weave should be handled a little differently from those of other stitches. When ending a thread, take the needle to the back as if to finish the stitch. Weave the needle under the woven threads of the backing so that the pattern is not altered. Begin the new strand of yarn by weaving it under the strands at a right angle to the ended strand. This keeps the back neat and also prevents too much bulk in one place on the back. If the yarn is ended and started correctly, the only indication of a new thread will be the tiny ends showing on the reverse side. Faulty ending is another cause of those diagonal shadows so often found in pieces worked in the basket weave stitch.

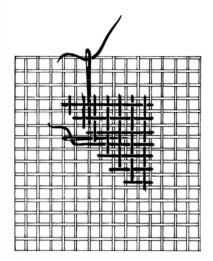

Correct method for fastening ends when Basketweave stitch is used. *(See text.)*

THE DIAGONAL STITCH

The diagonal stitch is the least used of the stitching techniques that create the tent stitch. It is a very fast stitch to work since it is the easy row of the basket weave stitch repeated again and again and the upward slanting row keeps the hand in the most natural working position. The stitch does not stretch the canvas badly out of shape, nor does it require the attention that basket weave does as far as keeping the correct direction of the rows. The surface texture of the diagonal stitch is much smoother than that of the basket weave since all stitches are worked in the same direction. This is really a very good stitch. It has a firm, smooth, snag-proof surface; enough padding to make it long wearing; and the added advantage of being so easy to work.

The first row of the diagonal stitch is the longest row slanting upward across the canvas from the lower right corner to the upper left corner. The bottom triangle is worked first, then the canvas is turned completely around and the other half is finished. All rows must begin at the bottom of the canvas and be ended at the top of the row. This working method is part of the reason that this stitch is so fast and easy to do.

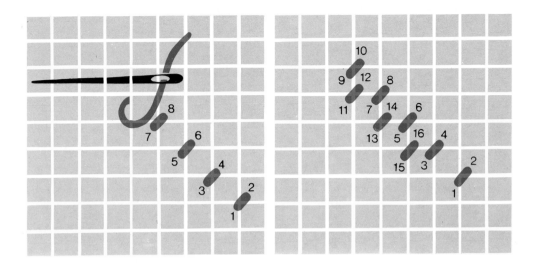

Begin by anchoring the yarn in the lower right corner of the canvas and bringing the needle up at 1 in the space for the first stitch. Following the chart, work up the row following the numbers and noting that the needle always passes horizontally under two vertical threads of the canvas. The numbered stitches on the first chart are those of the first row. The second chart is drawn to illustrate the way the stitches fit into the spaces to cover the canvas.

WORKING TENT STITCH BACKGROUNDS

To work the background of a piece on which the central motif is already stitched, start basket weave and continental stitches in the upper right corner. The horizontal half cross-stitch should be started in the upper left corner. Start the vertical half cross-stitch and diagonal stitches in the lower right.

Continental and horizontal half cross-stitches should be worked in long rows completely across the canvas until the design is reached. At this point, short rows are worked from the edges in to the design. It is better to do a few rows on each side of the design to keep the canvas from stretching unnecessarily. The small areas inside the design which are to be worked in the background color are also worked at this time. When the portion surrounding the design is completed, long rows are again worked all the way across the canvas to the bottom.

The basket weave stitch will form bias rows which get longer every row and finally reach the design. Being sure to keep the sequence of rows the same as you have been working, work around the design until the rows again

Mouse Picture. *This is an eighteenth-century American canvas embroidery picture. Worked in silk on linen, the stitching is very fine. The picture is done entirely in the tent stitch. The lovely soft colors complement the whimsical design.*
(Photo courtesy of the Smithsonian Institution)

meet on the left side of the design. Continue the long rows to the corner. (In the basket weave stitch, it is important that one upward row alternate with one downward row to prevent a diagonal striping across the canvas. If you are not sure of the direction in which the stitching should go, work a few stitches. Look at the weave on the wrong side. If the stitches are not right, the weave will not look right and you will know that you have to reverse the direction of the stitches. After one becomes more familiar with the stitch, it is obvious from the weave on the back which direction the stitching should go. This is something one learns from experience.)

The diagonal stitch is worked much like the basket weave stitch as far as directions for working around the design are concerned. This stitch begins in the lower right corner of the piece and the left side of the canvas is covered first. The piece is then turned around so that what was the bottom becomes the top and the remainder is worked.

The vertical half cross-stitch begins in the bottom right corner of the canvas and is worked in rows straight up the canvas. When the design is reached, short rows are worked top and bottom until long rows can again be worked on the left side of the design.

18th Century Sampler. *This early eighteenth-century sampler of animal motifs was worked in silk on a linen canvas. The colors are soft golds, greens, and blues.*
(Photo courtesy of the Smithsonian Institution)

6
THE FANCY NEEDLEPOINT STITCHES

The stitches in this chapter represent a broad cross-section of decorative needlepoint stitches. The finished stitches appearing in the photographs are followed by easy-to-read numbered diagrams wich show at a glance the path of the needle as it goes in and out of the canvas. The odd numbers represent the emerging needle, while the even ones indicate the places where the needle is inserted.

Follow the numbers in correct sequence to the ends of the rows. Where there are little tips that will aid in the working, they are included. Any descriptions and ideas for use which be helpful to the reader are also given.

Book of Common Prayer and Holy Bible. *Containing the geneology of the McCulloch family, the Bible is dated 1741, but the needlepoint cover was probably made in Ireland between 1740 and 1775. The needlepoint cover is worked in wool yarn on a linen canvas. The stitch is the cross-stitch. The background is a rich shade of red and the leaves and flowers are multi-colored.*

(Photo courtesy of the Henry Francis du Pont Winterthur Museum)

THE CROSS-STITCH

The cross-stitch is the same stitch that is used so extensively in many types of embroidery. As a needlepoint stitch it is also the basis for many other stitches and stitch variations. Historically, the cross-stitch was much more favored than it is today, but it remains a very decorative and useful stitch.

When working the cross you must take care to cross all the stitches in the same direction to ensure a smooth appearance. To do this work all the bottom stitches from left to right and cross them with the top stitches on the return journey as shown in the diagram. As shown here in both photograph and stitch chart, the cross-stitch has been worked over two threads of mono canvas. The height of the crosses can be increased to make an oblong cross. Although some consider this a separate stitch, it is merely a variation possible with many stitches and does not always merit illustration.

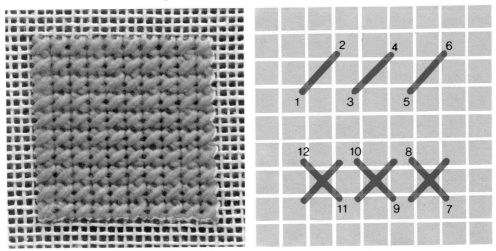

CROSS STITCH TRAMÉ

This stitch consists of laying one long (tramé) thread and working cross stitches over it. The tramé threads serve to raise the stitches and emphasize the pattern. Vary the lengths of the tramé threads to prevent a shadow from emerging.

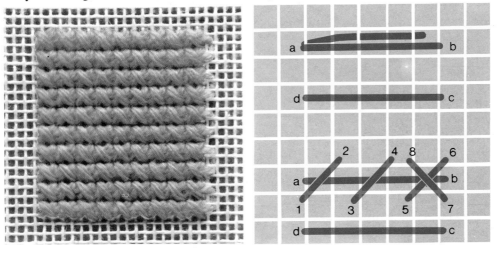

THE UPRIGHT CROSS-STITCH

The surface of the upright cross-stitch is very smooth and hard. The grained effect is very attractive. Unlike the cross-stitch, each cross should be completed before going on to the next one. The stitch can be worked in both directions, so there is no need to turn the canvas to work successive rows. All should cross in the same direction for a good appearance.

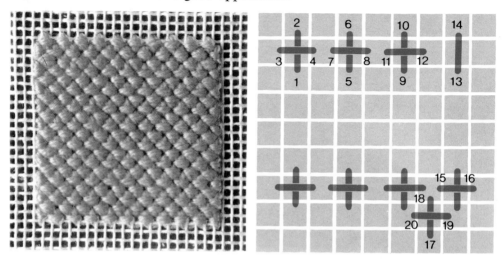

THE THREE-STITCH CROSS

This interesting variation of the cross-stitch is worked in rows beginning at the bottom right and working upward. As with all the cross-stitches, keep the same sequence of stitches throughout to achieve an even effect.

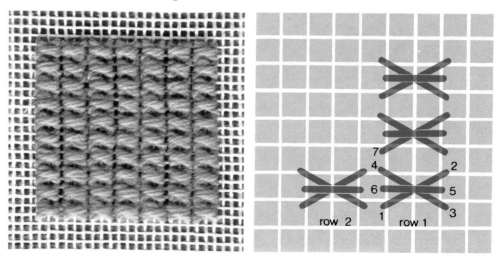

OBLONG CROSS WITH BACK STITCH

This stitch is actually a combination of an elongated cross-stitch overstitched with backstitches. The latter serve to tie down the long cross-stitches and add durability. It is shown here worked over four threads, but can also be worked over two threads to make a firmer ground. For an interesting variation, you can work the backstitches in a constrasting color, in which case, you would first work all the cross-stitches, then change colors and work the backstitches. If desired, you can also work backstitches between rows for a decorative effect.

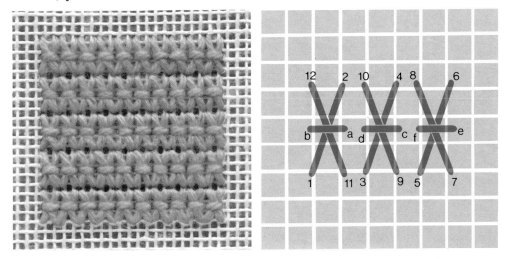

ITALIAN THREE-SIDED CROSS-STITCH

Shown here worked over four threads of canvas, this stitch does not cover the canvas adequately. The enlargement, however, does make it easier to see the pattern and the working method. As shown, the stitch can be worked over a ground of tent stitches to create a difference in texture. Or the size of the stitch can be reduced to two threads and a tight ground stitch results. The Italian three-sided cross-stitch looks like a complicated pattern stitch, but a rhythm quickly develops, which makes the stitching easy.

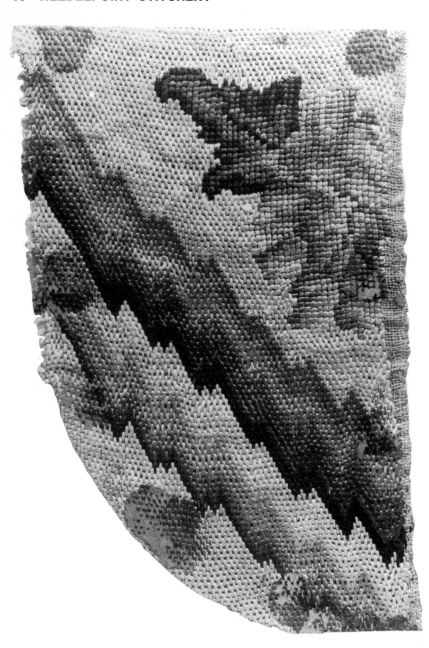

Italian Embroidery. *Fragment of an eighteenth-century embroidery worked entirely in silk in tones of yellow, green, and black.*
(Photo courtesy of the Metropolitan Museum of Art)

Needlepoint Rug. *This beautiful needlepoint carpet is English in origin and is from the period between 1800 and 1830. Worked in wool on canvas, the rug measures 117" x 91" and it is theorized that it may have been cut down from a larger piece at some time. The stitch is the cross-stitch. The background is cream with a fine cross-hatched design of maroon worked over it. This ground is broken by narrow, regular stripes of green with double sawtooth edges. Between the stripes there are stylized leafy and floral vines in several shades of green.*
(Photo courtesy of the Henry Francis du Pont Winterthur Museum)

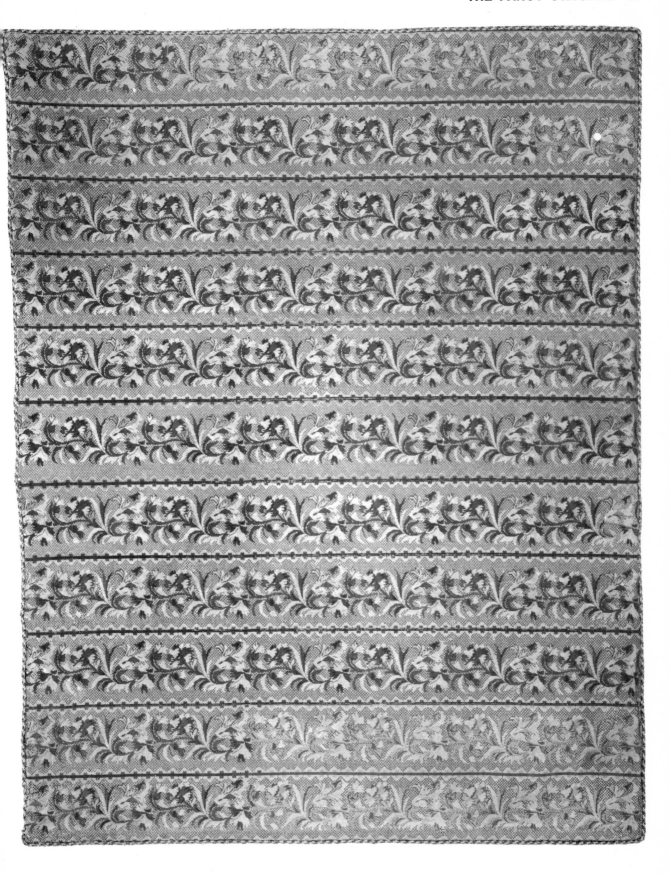

THE DIAGONAL CROSS-STITCH

This distinctive cross-stitch is worked in diagonal rows upward across the canvas. The fact that all the stitches are made in the same sequence emphasizes the pattern. Again, this stitch has been enlarged by working it over four threads to make the pattern easier to see. To use the diagonal cross-stitch as a background or a stitch covering the canvas completely, work over two threads. Be sure that your yarn is not too thick for this stitch, for when there are this many crosses, the stitches quickly become very crowded and appear blurred.

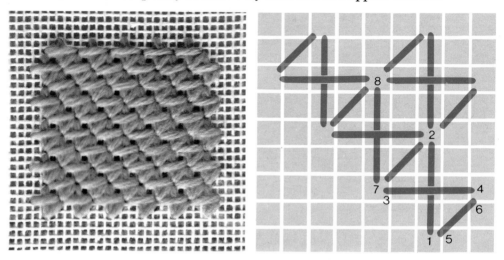

THE MONTENEGRIN CROSS-STITCH

This is still another of the cross-stitch variations, again enlarged to make the intricate pattern of interlaced stitches more easily seen. Actually, the stitches are very simple, but, as in all cross-stitches, they should cross in the same direction. To give a finished appearance to an area worked in the Montenegrin cross-stitch, begin and end each row with a single upright stitch.

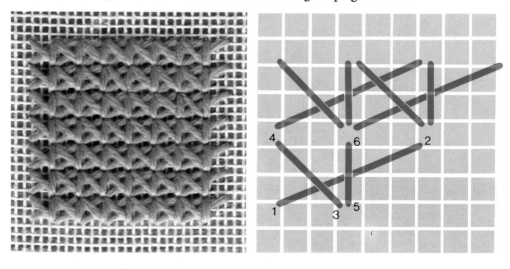

SMYRNA CROSS-STITCH

This stitch, actually a combination of cross-stitch and upright crosses, has a neat, snag-proof surface of little raised crosses. Complete each cross before moving on to the next one. Establish a pattern of stitch sequence in the very beginning and you will find that the stitches go in almost automatically. Note that the stitch can also be worked over four threads in which case you would have to adjust for curves, angles and squared-off areas by taking small horizontal, vertical or slanting stitches wherever necessary.

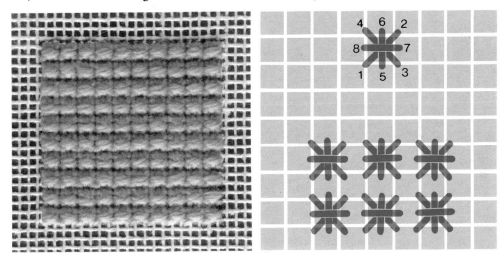

THE DOUBLE STRAIGHT CROSS-STITCH

The development of a stitch is always interesting. This one begins with an upright cross worked over four threads. A smaller cross over two mesh holds it down and fills in all the spaces very neatly. This is a slightly raised diamond-shaped stitch that is very attractive.

Choosing the proper yarn for this stitch will call for you to use your good judgment. Experiment a bit before making a final selection, for if the yarn is too heavy, the entire pattern effect will be lost.

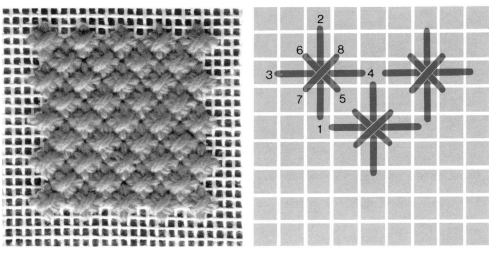

THE RICE STITCH

Although very tedious to work, the rice stitch does have a very good, smooth surface and a most attractive texture and pattern. It is basically the cross-stitch with a small diagonal stitch tying down the four corners. It is interesting to make the crosses of one color and to use a contrasting color to tie down the corners. The diagram shows the steps in forming the crosses and, finally, the entire process.

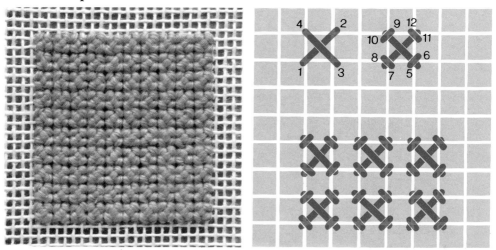

THE UPRIGHT GOBELIN STITCH OR STRAIGHT GOBELIN

This stitch can be worked over a varying number of threads, depending on how wide a stripe of stitches is desired. Any number of threads from two to six is appropriate, but remember that the longer the stitches, the more problem with snagging. The upright Gobelin stitch produces very pronounced horizontal rows of pattern, but covers ground very quickly and is the kind of background stitch that adds texture, but does not overpower the design itself. When working these vertical stitches, work with a little looser tension than normal so that the yarn can "fluff" out and cover the canvas better.

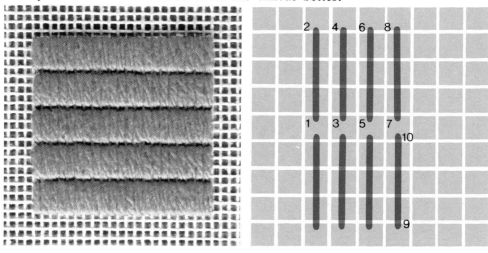

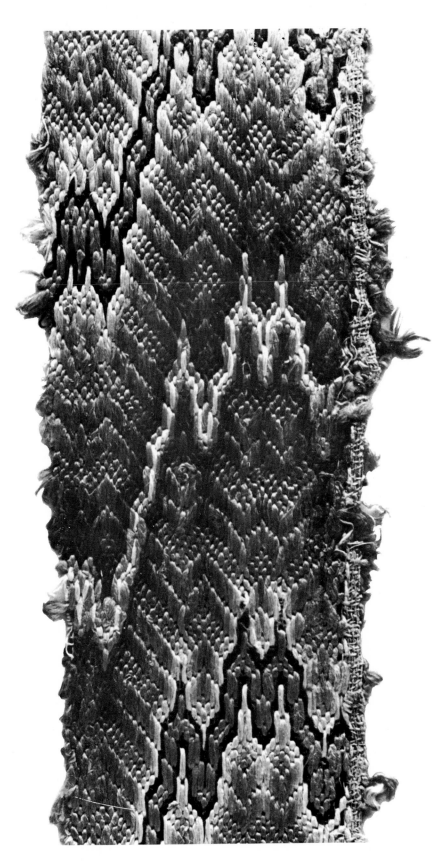

Italian Embroidery. *A beautiful example of seventeenth- and eighteenth-century Italian embroidery in silk, this pattern was worked in Gobelin stitches in soft shades of rose and green on a cream-colored background.*
(Photo courtesy of the Metropolitan Museum of Art)

SLANTING GOBELIN

This stitch was first used to imitate old seventeenth-century tapestries originally worked on very fine linen. It looks particularly beautiful when worked in several colors. When completed, it produces a slightly ridged effect that is good for working backgrounds and area filling. The Gobelin stitch is worked here so that it slants across one vertical thread of the canvas. The slight slant of the stitches changes the pattern only slightly, thus the stitch as the same virtues as the upright Gobelin.

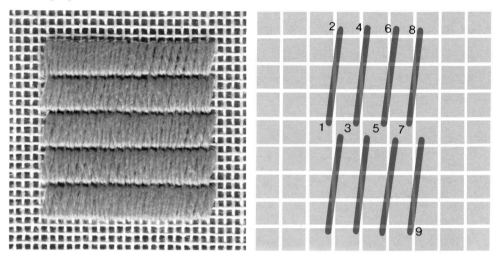

THE ENCROACHING GOBELIN STITCH

The slanting Gobelin stitch is worked here so that the top of each stitch reaches one thread above the bottom of each stitch in the row above. This creates an interwoven pattern and, for this reason, this stitch is ofen referred to as the "interlocking Gobelin." The surface of this stitch is a little firmer than that of either the straight or slanted Gobelin. At times the direction of the slant of the stitches is reversed to give the illusion of movement in the other direction.

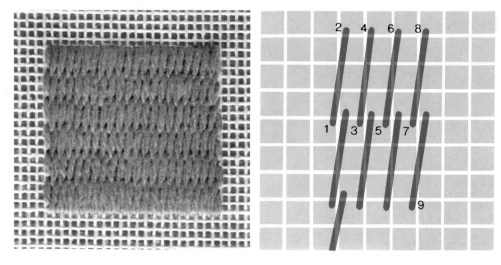

THE PLAITED GOBELIN STITCH

An interesting variation of the Gobelin stitch is achieved by reversing the slant of the stitches as well as interlocking them. This gives a good, smooth surface and a texture that does not have a definite direction. It is an especially good stitch to use for rugs or other heavy-duty items as it works up quickly and the interlocking stitches make it very strong.

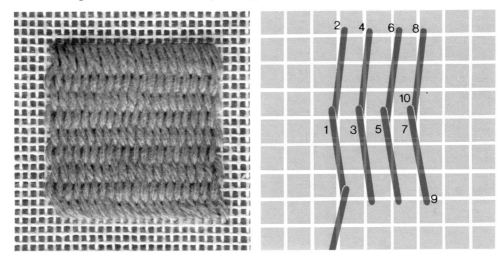

PARISIAN STITCH

The Parisian stitch is similar to the Upright Gobelin stitch worked in a pattern of alternating long and short stitches. You will find that it is extremely quick and easy to do and it produces an excellent textured background which does not "fight" the main design in any way.

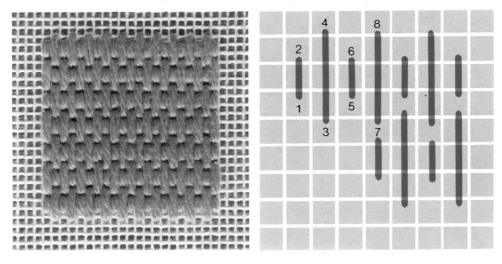

THE BRICK STITCH

The brick stitch is the upright Gobelin again; this time arranged so that the stitches are alternately two threads up and two down, creating the "brick" pattern. This stitch works very quickly and the stitches should be worked fairly loosely so that the canvas will be covered. The length of the stitches can be varied according to the effect desired. Shown on the chart they are only two threads high, but work beautifully four threads high and can be lengthened up to six stitches if a more elongated pattern is needed.

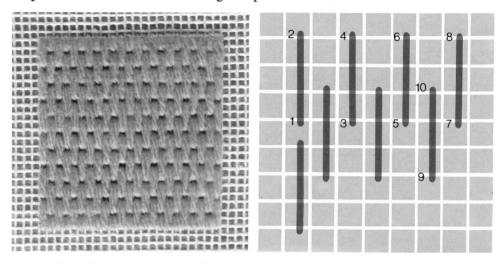

Spanish Embroidery. *This is an eighteenth-century Spanish border worked in silk. The gold background is worked entirely in the brick stitch. Parts of the design have been worked so that the stitches are horizontal. All of the design areas are outlined in brown outline stitch.*
(Photo courtesy of the Metropolitan Museum of Art)

HUNGARIAN STITCH

The Hungarian stitch is one of the oldest in needlepoint. Three upright Gobelin stitches, this time arranged in a group consisting of two short and one long stitch, create a diamond shaped pattern. This is a very popular stitch because it works up very quickly and requires a minimum of concentration after the first row has been worked. Stitched in one color, it produces a nice area covering. If you work by rows in two, three or more colors, it will result in an attractive textured look.

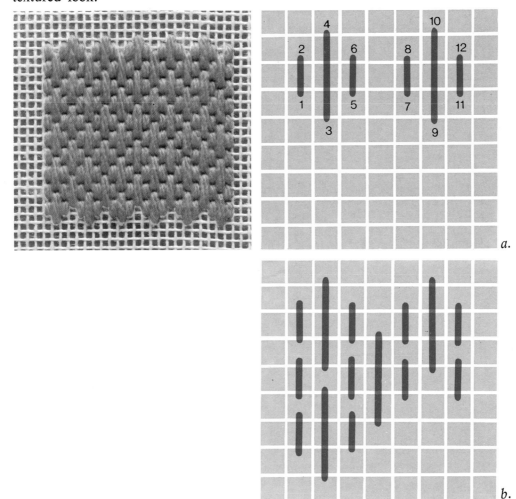

a.

b.

THE BARGELLO STITCH OR FLAME STITCH

In the bargello stitch the upright Gobelin stitches are worked in steps up and down the row to create the traditional flame pattern. When worked in several shades of one color, the stitches reveal the lovely flame patterns. This simple stitch can be placed on the canvas to form many beautiful patterns, as discussed more fully in Chapter 8.

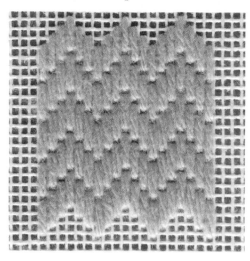

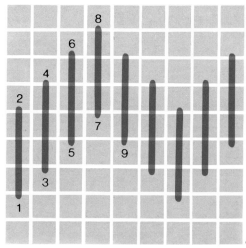

a.

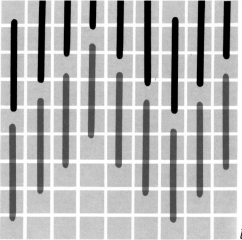

b.

THE OLD FLORENTINE STITCH

The old Florentine stitch is a very loose one since the longest stitches must be equal in length to three of the shorter side stitches. (If the short stitches are two threads high, the long ones must be six. If the short stitches are three threads high, they must be paired with stitches nine threads high.) The stitches are, again, the simple upright Gobelin.

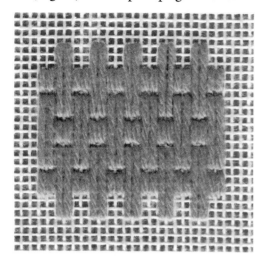
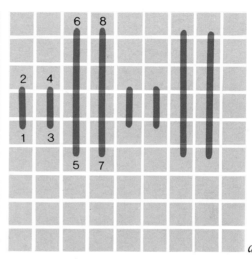

a.

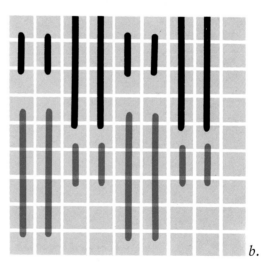

b.

SCOTCH STITCH

The Scotch stitch is one of the best known and most widely used of the decorative needlepoint stitches. This stitch has many variations and decorative possibilities and is equally useful when working borders, backgrounds, or simple area filling. You'll find that the stitch is fun to experiment with, both with color and placement of stitches, but keep in mind that it does distort the canvas somewhat. As shown in the diagram, the stitch has ben worked over a square of three threads of canvas. A larger square of pattern is made by making one more long stitch in the center before decreasing to the smaller stitches in the sequences.

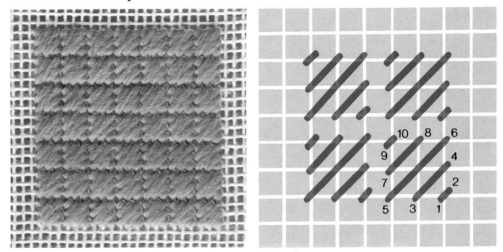

THE SCOTCH STITCH VARIATION

The Scotch squares are worked with one thread left open between them. The single stitch outline is then worked in one of the tent stitches in either the same color or a contrasting one.

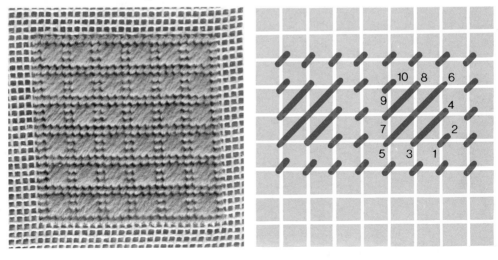

THE CHECKER STITCH

Squares of both Scotch and tent stitches alternate to make a checkerboard pattern. This variation is shown worked in contrasting colors, but it is equally attractive in one color only. Because the reader already knows the method of working both stitches, no numbers are included on the chart. Although you can use any of the tent stitch methods in chapter 5, many needlepointers find the basket weave stitch the most convenient as it does not distort the canvas as much and is easy to work diagonally.

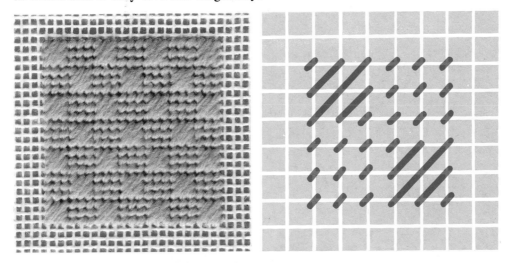

THE CROSSED SCOTCH STITCH

To form the crossed Scotch stitch, the first and last stitch of the square is omitted. Then a long stitch in the opposite direction is placed in the vacant spaces, which gives the crossed appearance. The end result is a rich and beautiful textured appearance that looks particularly good on large-mesh canvas.

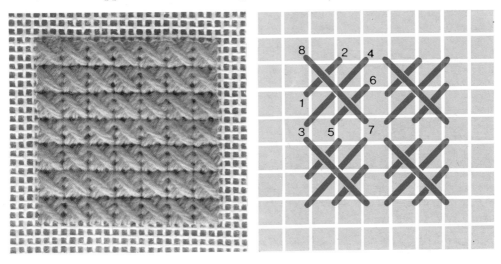

THE WOVEN SCOTCH STITCH

This Scotch stitch variation is similar to the crossed Scotch stitch except that the final stitch is actually woven through the Scotch stitch base rather than crossing over it.   Work in the woven stitch in the same or contrasting yarn for different looks.

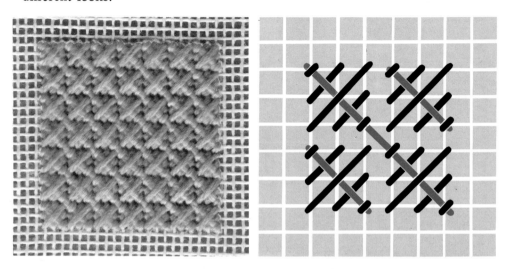

THE DIAGONAL SCOTCH STITCH

Placed on the canvas in diagonal rows, the Scotch stitch takes on a different look.   Notice that the small tent stitch that is the first and last stitch of each group is shared by the adjoining group of stitches.   The predominating pattern here is a diagonal line rather than the regular little squares of te Scotch stitch.

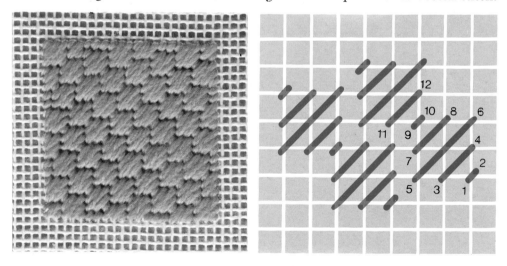

THE MOORISH STITCH

The Moorish stitch is the diagonal Scotch stitch with a row of tent stitches outlining the rows. The smaller stitches make the rows of diagonal Scotch stitches stand out and accent the diagonal pattern. Worked in two colors this stitch can be very showy. Begin working in the lower right corner and work upward diagonally. Place the Scotch stitch first and then outline with the tent stitches. The chart is not numbered since the diagonal Scotch stitch is shown above.

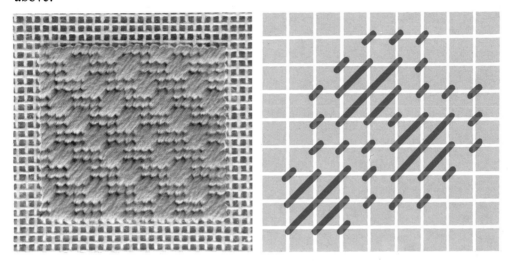

MOSAIC STITCH

The Mosaic stitch is actually a miniature version of the Scotch stitch, using three stitches—two short and one long—instead of five. It produces a neat, flat textured pattern that does not interfere with a central design, which makes it a good background stitch. Because all of the stitches are diagonal, there is usually a lot of canvas distortion, but this is easily corrected in blocking.

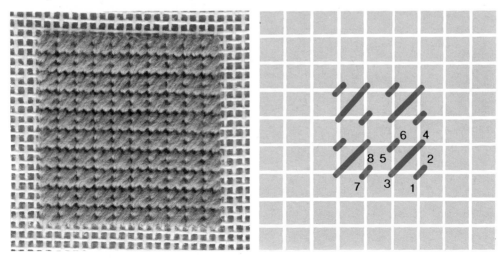

Owl Book Jacket.   *This book jacket is enlivened by a wise little owl worked in the tent stitch against a background of sky worked in the mosaic stitch. (Photo courtesy of Nina Needlepoint)*

THE DIAGONAL MOSAIC STITCH

Worked diagonally on the canvas, the mosaic has a very different appearance.
It is easiest to work the diagonal rows upward from the lower right to the
upper left of the canvas.

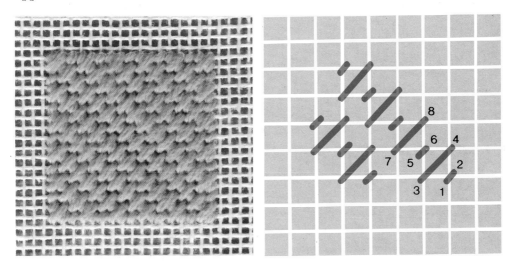

KALEM STITCH

Originally, the Kalem stitch was designed to resemble the tapestry weaving
used for rugs. It is a versatile stitch found in many museum pieces. Although
it is no longer used as widely today, it remains an excellent stitch for rugs
and upholstered pieces due to its well-padded back. If you look closely, you
will see that the stitch which is worked in vertical rows, produces a pattern that
resembles knitting.

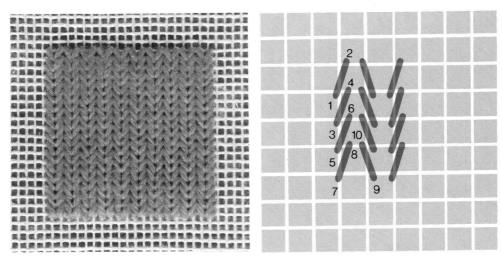

THE CASHMERE STITCH

It is easy to see that the cashmere stitch is the mosaic stitch with one long stitch added. The pattern is thus changed from one of little squares to one of small oblong blocks. Also quick to work up, the cashmere stitch is very neat and attractive for both detail work and background. The stitch does end up distorting the canvas quite a bit, so it's a good idea to have the exact outline of the design on a piece of paper before you start stitching. It will be invaluable later on in blocking.

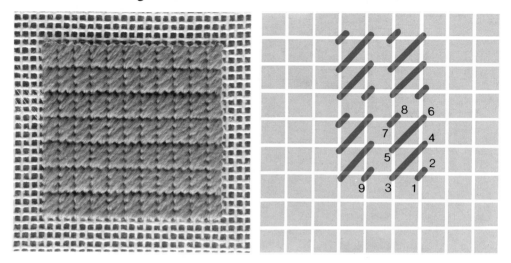

THE DIAGONAL CASHMERE STITCH

Again we see how working a stitch on the diagonal of the canvas can change its overall appearance. This version of the cashmere stitch has a softer look since the pattern of the oblong blocks is not as definite as in the regular cashmere.

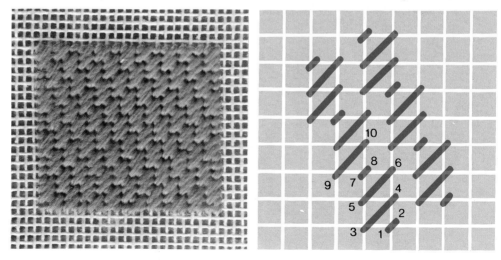

THE CASHMERE VARIATION

Strong vertical stripes are formed by working the cashmere stitch straight up the row unbroken by the small stitch that normally begins and ends each group of stitches. The numbered row on the diagram shows how a small stitch begins and ends the row.

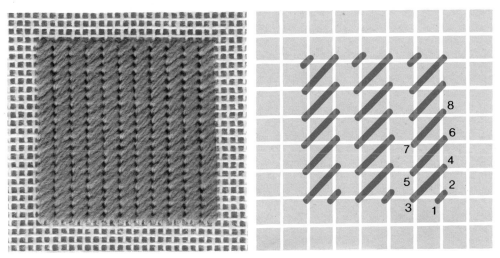

THE ENCROACHING OBLIQUE STITCH

Another good background stitch is the encroaching oblique stitch. The interlocking stitches have a good firm texture, but they do not create a bold pattern effect. The surface of this stitch is very attractive and makes a pleasant change from the tent stitch.

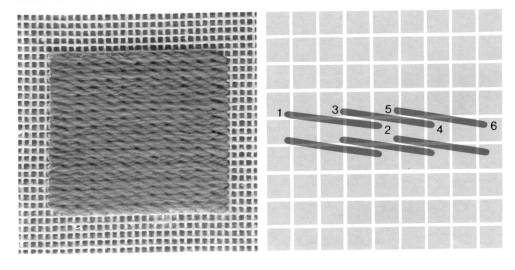

THE KNITTING STITCH

The knitting stitch looks very much like the kalem stitch except that it is worked horizontally on the canvas. The appearance and the surface texture are as good as the kalem stitch, but because of the working method, the backing is not as heavy. The first row is worked across the canvas from the left. The second row is worked in the return direction without turning the canvas.

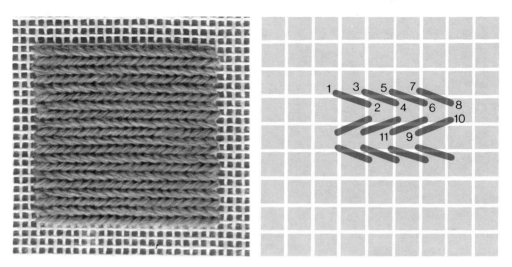

SPANISH PLAIT

This is a most attractive stitch with a tightly woven, ridged appearance. The horizontal rows actually look like tiny raised braids. Although the first few stitches require a little thought, once the rhythm of working is established, the rest go quickly. Keep the tension even to assure a smooth, braided appearance. You should also note that the back of the canvas is well-covered with this stitch which makes it a suitable choice for heavy-duty items.

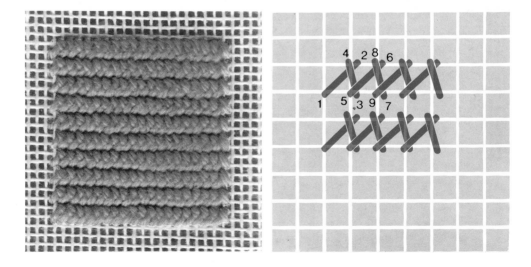

THE PLAITED ALGERIAN STITCH

Here a simple bit of stitching creates a pattern that looks very complicated. It is better to work this row beginning at the left side of the canvas, working all the way across the row, ending the yarn, and beginning the new row again at the left side. This saves time and prevents getting lost in the stitching.

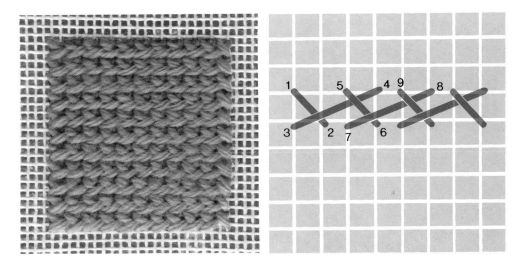

THE GREEK STITCH

At first glance, the Greek stitch looks like the Algerian plait, but the stitching is slightly different and examination reveals differences in appearance. Begin at the left side of the row and work to the end. Turn the canvas to return.

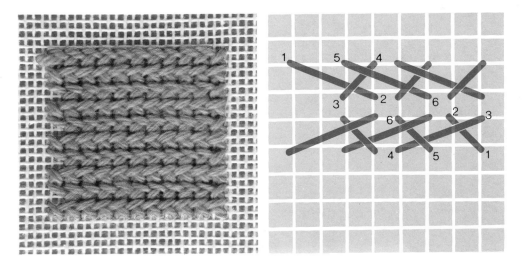

PLAITED STITCH

The plaited stitch is another of the very old needlepoint stitches. It is used very rarely today which is a bit sad since it is one of the prettiest of all needlepoint stitches. It is perfect both for backgrounds and small design areas. Although it looks rather complicated, it is not really difficult to work. Begin all rows at the top and work down. Note how successive rows interlock to form the plaited look.

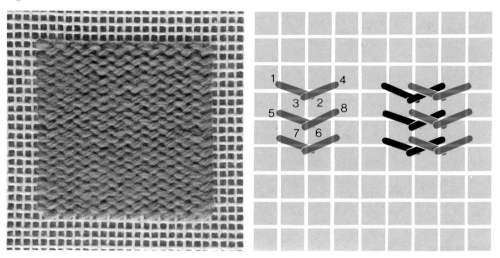

TURKEY WORK

This is one of the oldest rug-making stitches known. Turkey work loops can be cut, as shown in the lower half of the stitch sample, or left untrimmed, as shown in the top section. This allows for two different looks from one stitch. Cut loops make very realistic animals and some plants, for example a cattail or dandelion head. A rabbit worked in flat stitches with a little round pompon tail of clipped turkey work is very appealing. If you are planning to cut the loops, do remember to stitch first and cut later so the resulting tufts will be uniform in size.

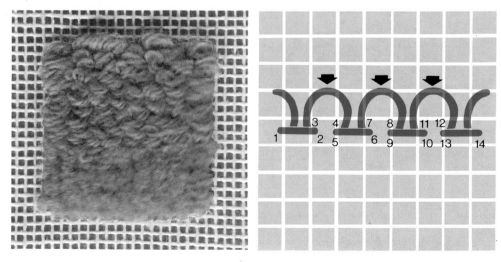

Cromwellian-Type Side Chair.
The chair itself was probably made in England between the years 1650-1690. The turkey work upholstery is English and also dates from about 1675. The seat and back are upholstered in woolen turkey work panels with a dark blue and brown background and an allover pattern of leafy flowers in polychrome colors. The upholstery is held in place with brass tacks.
(Photo courtesy of the Henry Francis du Pont Winterthur Museum)

THE HERRINGBONE STITCH

This is one of several versions of the herringbone stitch that can be used for needlepoint. It is most effective used as a border or frame. It is also very beautiful worked in several shades of one color for a more three-dimensional look.

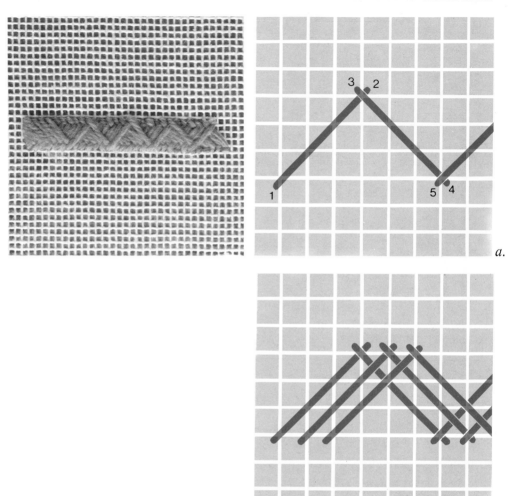

a.

b.

THE MILANESE STITCH

This stitch is very decorative, but it is practical only where special effect is important. It is interesting to work and does cover ground quickly. Begin at the top left of the area and work the row of arrowheads downward diagonally. Turn the canvas and work back, fitting the reversed arrows into the spaces. This stitch really distorts the canvas, so be sure to outline the design area on a piece of paper before stitching to help you later in blocking.

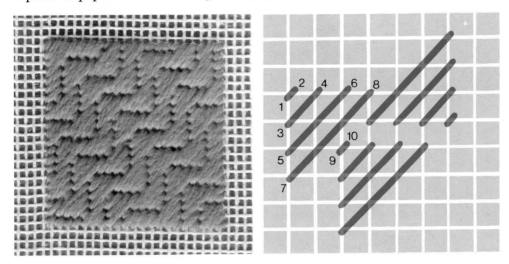

THE JACQUARD STITCH

The stitches of the jacquard stitch are placed like those of the Byzantine, but the width of the stitches is varied: a wide row alternates with a narrow row. This varies the texture. Jacquard worked in one color is interesting. In two or more colors, it creates its own bold pattern. For an unusual and effective background, work this stitch with two different kinds of yarn—one for the long stitches, another for the short ones—in the same color.

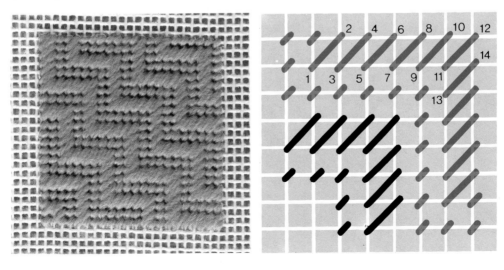

THE BYZANTINE STITCH

Large areas covered in Byzantine stitch have a look similar to brocade. The regular steps of the pattern make a very interesting background, but the stitch can be used imaginatively for special effects also. The stitch is the slanting Gobelin, and the arrangement can be changed to make the steps deeper or the stitches can be shortened to make a narrower stripe.

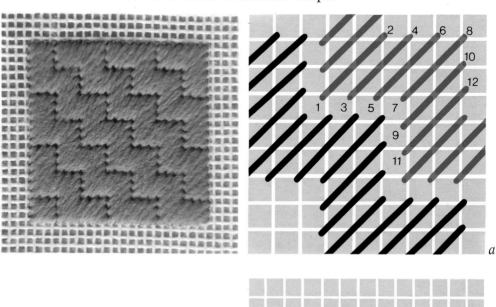

a.

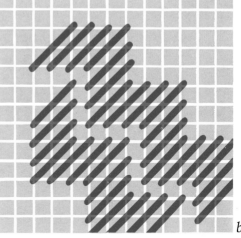

b.

ORIENTAL STITCH

This stitch is actually and adaptation of an old embroidery pattern. The small scale of the worked sample cannot do justice to the intricacies of the oriental stitch. The stitch is worked in two steps. The arrowheads are first worked (numbers 1 through 8 on the stitch chart). Then the three slanting stitches on either side (*a* through *f* on the stitch chart) are added. This stitch is fancy enough to be used by itself, but it is not easy enough to maneuver to make it practical to use in small design areas. Try working the arrowheads and the other pattern in contrasting colors for an unusual variation.

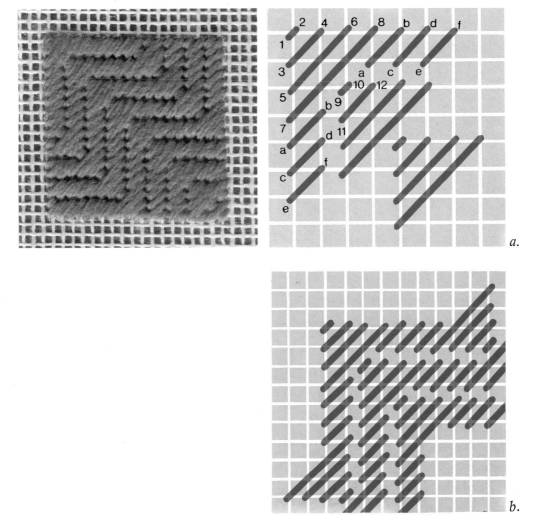

a.

b.

THE FERN STITCH

The fern stitch forms a raised braid that constitutes a very definite vertical stripe. All rows must be worked from the top. Keep an even tension as you work so the braid will be neat and smooth.

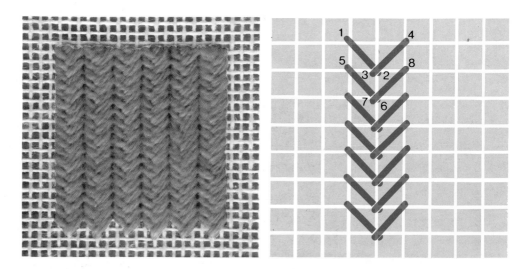

THE STEM STITCH

The stem stitch is worked in two steps. First the slanting stitches are placed (numbered on the stitch diagram) These are worked in two rows slanting in opposite directions. Beginning at the top, a row of backstitches is placed where the slanting stitches meet. The backstitches can be worked in a contrasting color to add interest. It may be necessary to cut down on the thickness of the yarn used for the backstitches.

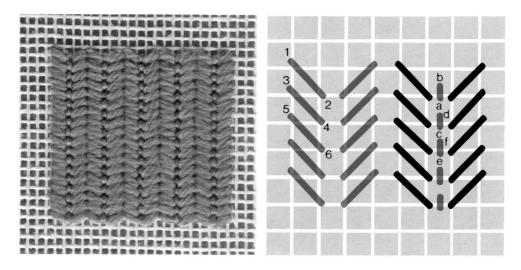

FLY STITCH

The fly stitch is actually an embroidery stitch which has been adapted for canvas work. It has an overall appearance similar to the stem stitch, but it is worked in one operation. It can be really attractive when stitched as a leaf, and makes lovely borders too. All rows are worked down from the top. This stitch is worked like the familiar lazy daisy embroidery stitch but open at the top. The numbered diagram at the top of the chart shows the yarn looped below the needle. The drawing at the bottom of the chart shows the formation of the small tie-down stitch.

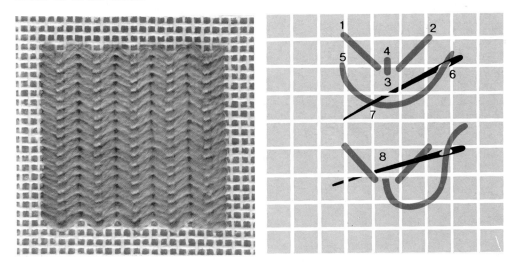

THE FISHBONE STITCH

The fishbone is a long slanting stitch tied down at the end by a smaller stitch worked over the very end. The slant of the stitches alternates in successive rows. Work the long stitch and its small tie-down stitch before making the next long stitch. Note that although the fishbone stitch can be worked on mono canvas, it is easier to work and looks much better done on penelope canvas.

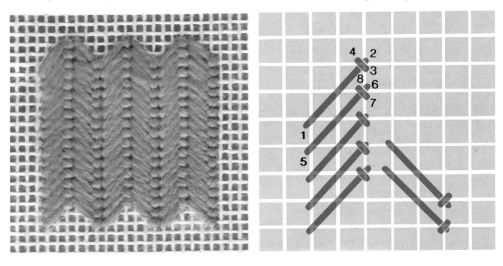

THE KNOTTED STITCH

The knotted stitch is a long slanting stitch tied down at the center with a short slanting stitch. This stitch forms a very smooth, hard surface and a very interesting pattern. Because it is a tie-down stitch, the knotted stitch is a little slow to work. However, it is attractive enough to make this worthwhile. You can use the stitch for shading because of the encroaching rows. Note also that this is a nice stitch to use on rug canvas.

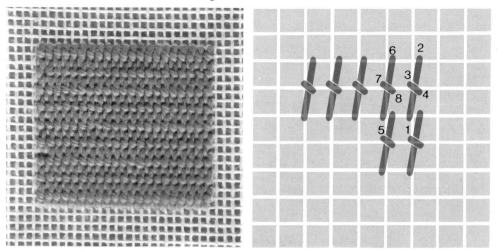

THE WEB STITCH

The web stitch can be a very time-consuming stitch, but there is no stitch that will produce a harder, longer-wearing surface. It is worked by laying long diagonal tramé threads over the threads of the canvas and fastening the tramé with a small stitch across every intersection of the canvas.

Working the web stitch can be speeded up if the tramé thread (as on the chart) is laid and the diagonal stitch is used for working the tie-down stitches. One row of tramé should be laid and the diagonal stitch worked over it before the next tramé is worked. An interesting tweed results if contrasting colors are used for the tramé and for the diagonal stitches.

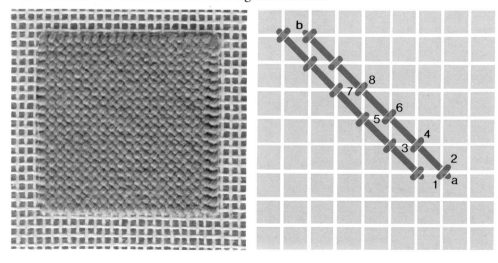

THE FRENCH STITCH

Another tied stitch is the French stitch. This one consists of two upright stitches worked into the same mesh of the canvas. Each stitch is then tied separately with a short stitch at the center. This is an attractive stitch with a good smooth surface. It can be used almost for almost anything—from area filling and backgrounds to rugs. If you work it on the horizontal, it can be used for shading. Worked diagonally, you can make either stripes or zigzag lines.

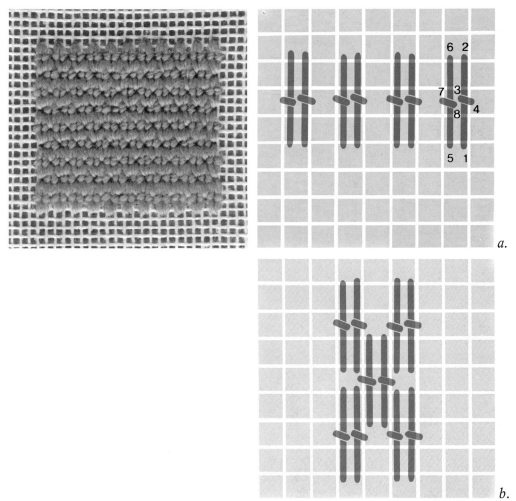

a.

b.

The Misses Henry Fragment
Worked entirely in the rococo stitch, this piece was probably intended as part of a pocketbook. The thread is silk and the work very fine. Beautiful shades of rose are used throughout. (Detail below.)
(Photo courtesy of the Smithsonian Institution)

THE ROCOCO STITCH

As shown here, the rococo stitch consists of a cluster of four stitches tied separately. These stitches are four threads in length, but they could be up to nine, since the little tie-down stitches hold the threads in place. The longer the threads, the larger the number of stitches in a cluster should be. The possibility of varying the size of the clusters thus makes different effects possible. It is best to make each long stitch and tie it into place before proceeding to the next stitch.

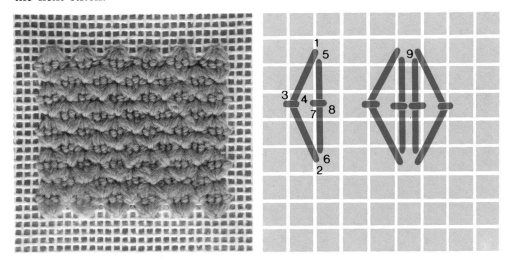

THE EYELET STITCH

This is a highly decorative stitch that combines well with other stitches, especially the square-shaped ones. Worked as shown, it takes twenty-four stitches to complete the grouping. It is wise to make all stitches in the same sequence. Only the uneven stitch numbers appear on the chart since all of the even-numbered stitches go down into the canvas in the central mesh, as indicated by the capital letter E.

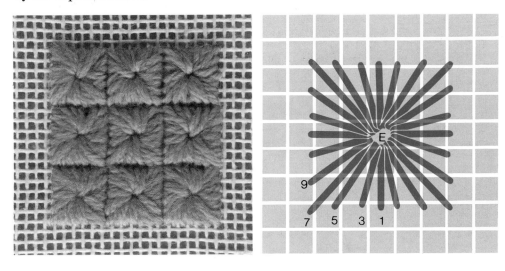

THE DIAMOND EYELET STITCH

Virtually the same as the eyelet stitch, this group of stitches is turned on its axis to form a diamond shape instead of a square. Again, only the odd-numbered stitches appear on the chart since all stitches downward into the canvas use the same central mesh, indicated by the capital letter E. Be aware that this stitch uses a lot of yarn and that yarn choice as well as quantity is important. With so many stitches inserted in the same mesh, the yarn must be fine enough to fit easily in the central mesh, but heavy enough to cover the single meshes at the outer edges. It's probably a good idea to work a practice piece before choosing yarn.

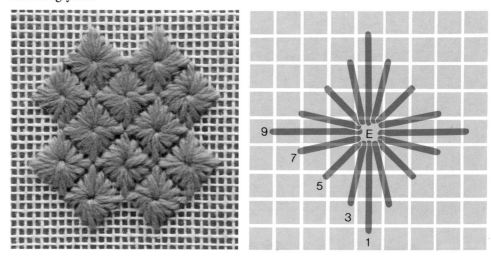

THE FAN STITCH

The fan stitch can be turned in either direction on the canvas. It is a stitch that seems to give an illusion of movement in the direction of the stitches. This stitch is more effective if all stitches in all fans are made in the same sequence. The even-numbered stitches are all inserted in the same mesh as indicated by the capital letter E.

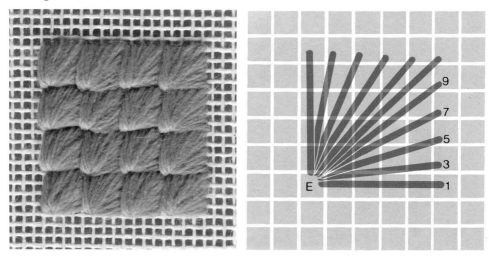

THE WHEAT SHEAF AND SHELL STITCH

The wheat sheaf stitch is a bundle of four upright stitches tied in the center to resemble a sheaf of wheat. The center section of the stitch sample photograph shows the stitches unadorned. The very bottom row shows the stitches with an upright cross in a contrasting color worked in the spaces between the groups of stitches. The top row of the photograph shows the shell version in which a contrasting color of yarn is threaded coil-fashion into the tie-down stitches.

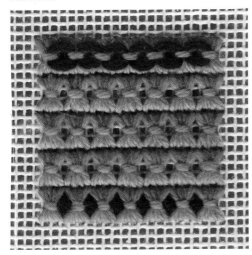

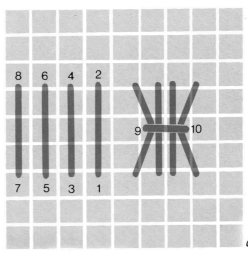

a.

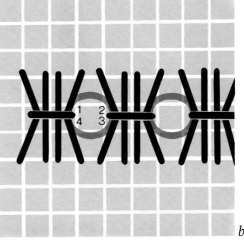

b.

THE LEAF STITCH

Although it looks hard to do, the leaf stitch is not really difficult. It has a look that is very unusual and very effective in a background. Note that diagram B does not represent a complete stitch, but is used to illustrate how a group of leaf stitches fit together.

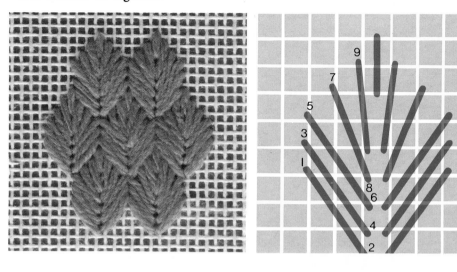

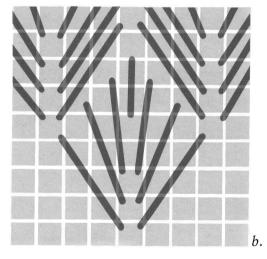

a.

b.

THE STAR STITCH

The star stitch makes a neat little square pattern, but it does not cover the canvas at all well. This can be remedied by working a backstitch in the spaces between the squares. The double star stitch, shown below, gives the same texture but covers the canvas completely. The even-numbered stitches, all inserted in the same mesh are represented by the capital letter E.

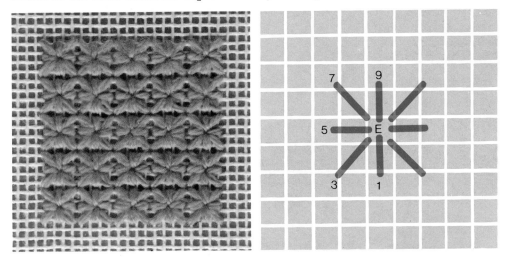

DOUBLE STAR STITCH

The addition of a few stitches solves the star stitch's problem of poor canvas coverage, but keeps the neat pattern intact. This is a very useful stitch because it is neat and flat, but at the same time highly decorative. The four stitches to the corners are worked first, then the small stitches between them, and finally the stitches perpendicular to the center.

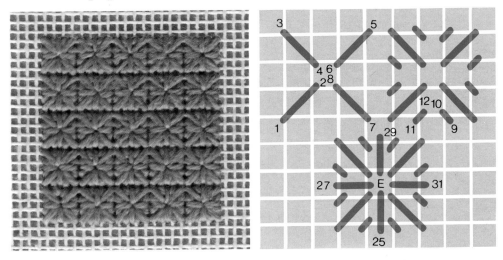

THE TRIANGLE STITCH

This stitch achieved its greatest popularity among the nineteenth-century Victorian needlepointers. It can be placed as shown or in straight rows to form a very decorative border. As a border, it is very good in two colors. The number of stitches can be increased or decreased as long as an uneven number of stitches is used.

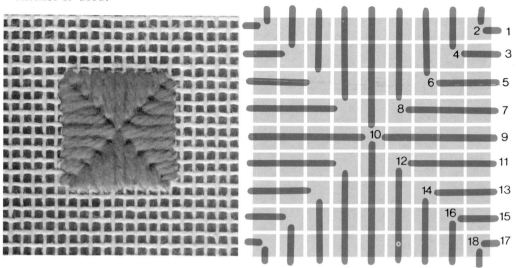

THE DOUBLE LEVIATHAN STITCH

If a raised texture is needed, this double leviathan stitch could be the answer. It is a high, but firm stitch. When working, establish a pattern of stitch sequence and maintain it for all squares. You can use this stitch alone or as an area filling, but it is not appropriate for background work.

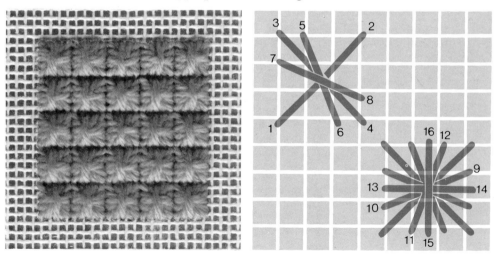

THE TRIPLE LEVIATHAN STITCH

Since this stitch does not work at all except as a decorative accent, it is not very useful. No needlepoint book, however, would be complete without it, so it is included for reference and as a curiosity. The twelve diagonal stitches to the center are worked first. The five upright crosses are worked last. The letter E indicates the even-numbered stitches. An interesting variation is to work the small upright cross stitches in a contrasting color.

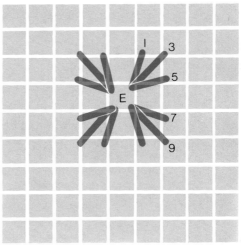

a.

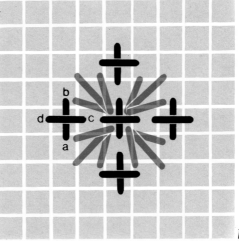

b.

7 DESIGN PORTFOLIO

The twelve designs included in the portfolio in this chapter were all created especially for this book. The photograph of each stitched piece is accompanied by a line drawing on a grid. The grids are there to enable you to reproduce the designs in any size you desire (see Chapter 2). In each case, the grid square shown is equal to 1/4-inch.

You will also see that the illustrations are keyed to indicate the stitches that were used to complete each piece. You can reproduce any of the designs as shown or adapt them to your own style and taste in color and stitches.

In many cases, you will find that embroidery stitches are used as accents in conjunction with the needlepoint stitches. For example in *Spring Garden* (page 124) some of the flower centers were given more interest by the use of French knots and the flowers themselves were given definition by couching the edges. The *Little Boy in Red Cap* (page 127) also uses a number of embroidery stitches to create amusing and imaginative effects. Although you have not encountered them as yet, all of the embroidery stitches used are discussed in Chapter 9 (page 142). Diagrams for working the stitches are also included. You will find as you become proficient in needlepoint, that embroidery stitches worked over needlepoint can really enhance a design and add just the touch of drama or distinction that you need. Don't be afraid to experiment with them and use them freely in all your future needlepoint projects.

A last word on these designs: Do try any or all of them that appeal to you, and do feel free to change or adapt them to suit your needs. As always the important thing to remember about needlepoint is that whether you are using a kit or designing your own, the ultimate goal is to enjoy yourself. Now, browse through this section and pick your pleasure.

Butterfly Rug. *A profusion of brilliant butterflies make a gay little rug or wall hanging. An original design by the author, this rug is available as a kit.*
(Photo courtesy of Columbia Minerva Corp.)

Key to the Stitches

a. Tent Stitch
b. French Knots
c. Brick Stitch
d. Encroaching Gobelin Stitch
e. Chain Stitch
f. Plaited Stitch
g. Jacquard Stitch

Jacobean Flower. *A flower reminiscent of those seen in typical Jacobean crewel embroideries is worked in a variety of needlepoint stitches with a French knot center. Background in jacquard stitch adds textural interest without interfering with the flower's importance.*

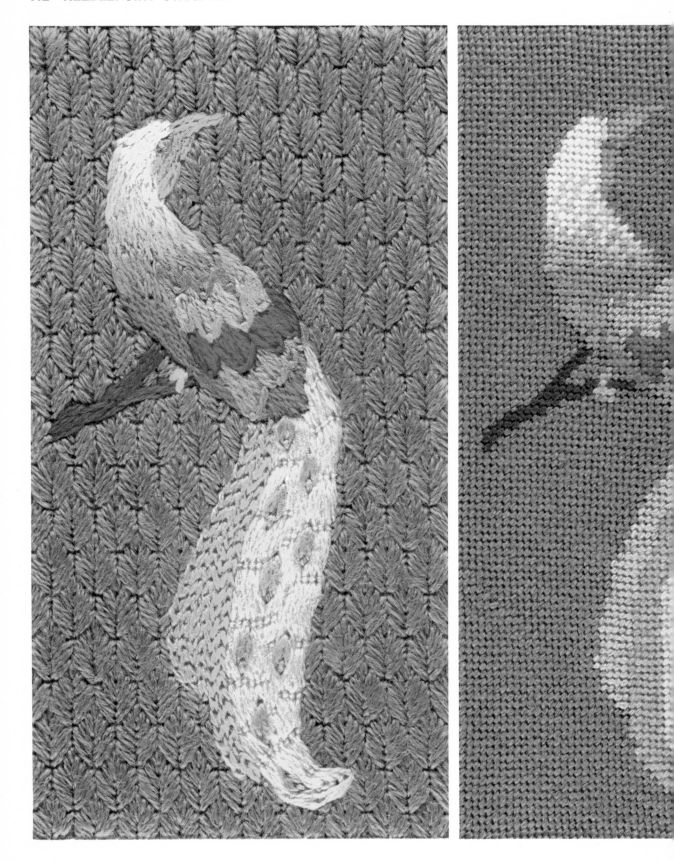

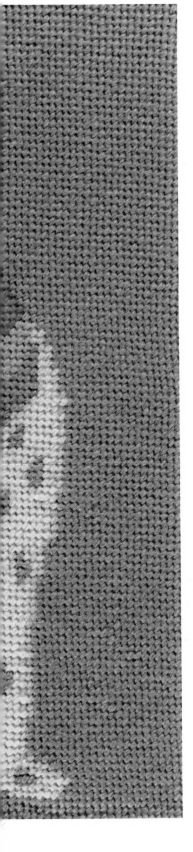

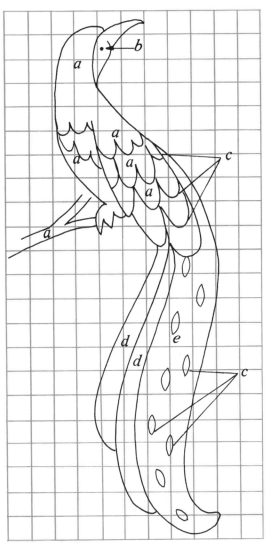

Key to the Stitches

a. *Straight Stitch*
b. *French Knots*
c. *Lazy Daisy Stitch*
d. *Chain Stitch*
e. *Couching*
f. *Background—Leaf Stitch*

Pair of Tropical Birds. *The bird pictures here were first encountered in Chapter 4 to illustrate the effectiveness of using fancy needlepoint stitches. Do go back to it as a reference. You can work the more ambitious design on the left or try working just the bird in fancy stitches on a plain tent stitch background. In either case, the end result will surely be satisfying.*

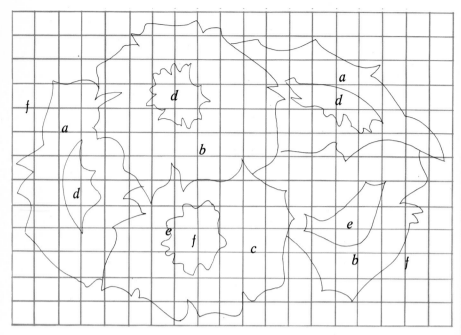

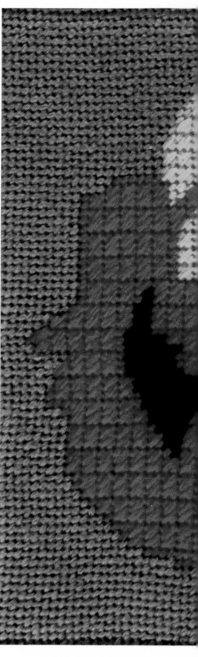

Key to the Stitches

a. Cashmere Stitch
b. Mosaic Stitch
c. Hungarian Stitch
d. Bullion Knots
e. French Knots
f. Tent Stitch

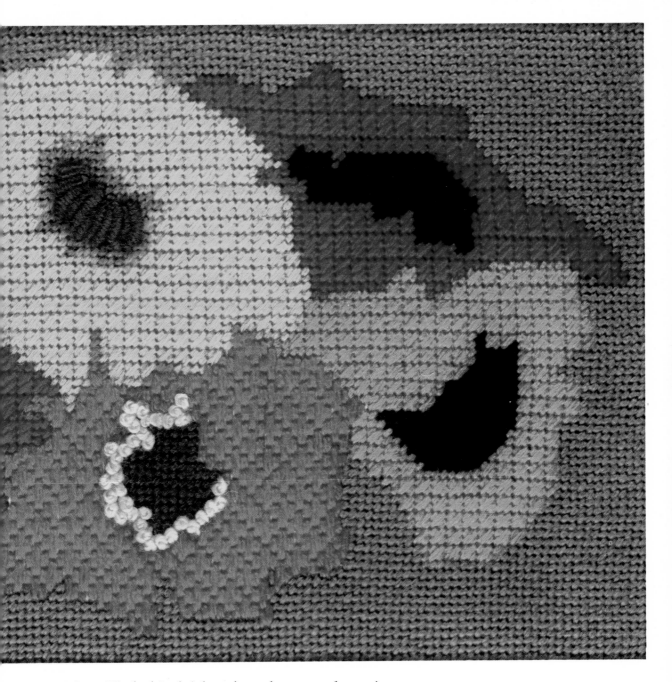

Poppies. *Worked in bright colors, the textured poppies seem to be lying on top of their contrastingly flat tent stitch background. This type of interplay is one of the biggest advantages of combining stitches.*

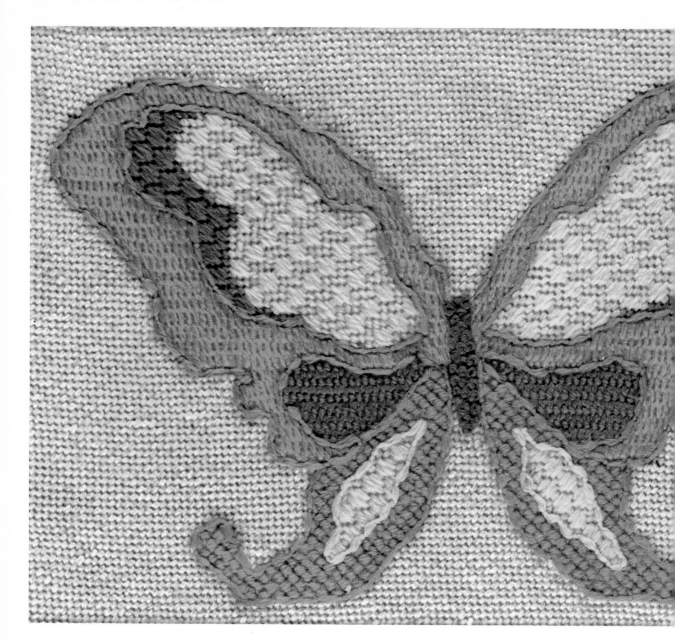

Butterfly. *A variety of novelty stitches are combined here to add interest to an otherwise uncomplicated design. Note that direction of stitching has been reversed on left side so that all stitches slant outward from the center.*

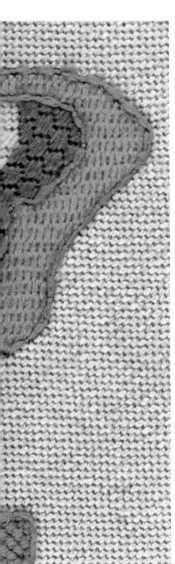

Key to the Stitches

a. *Diagonal Scotch Stitch*
b. *Moorish Stitch*
c. *Knotted Stitch*
d. *Encroaching Gobelin Stitch*
f. *Upright Cross-stitch*
g. *Couching*
h. *Basket Weave Stitch*
j. *French Knots*

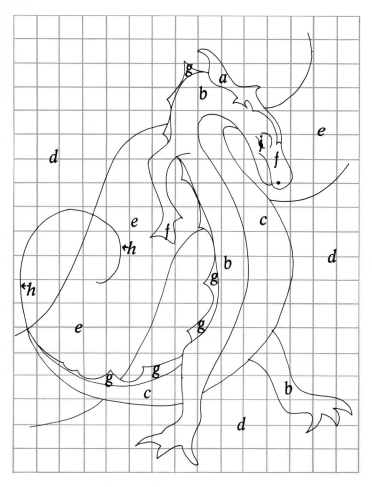

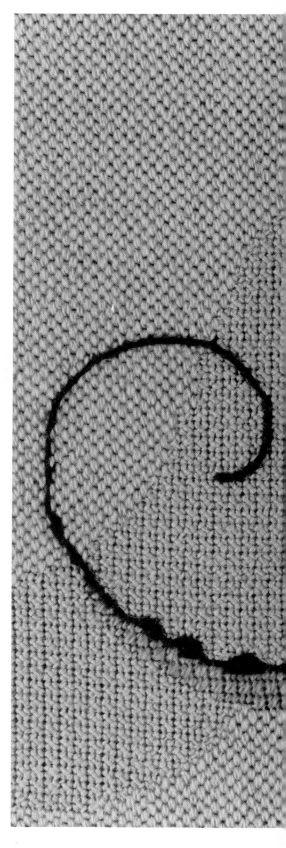

Key to the Stitches

a. Encroaching Gobelin Stitch
b. Double Straight Cross-stitch
c. Mosaic Stitch
d. Brick Stitch
e. Rice Stitch
f. Tent Stitch
g. Satin Stitch
h. Couching
j. French Knots

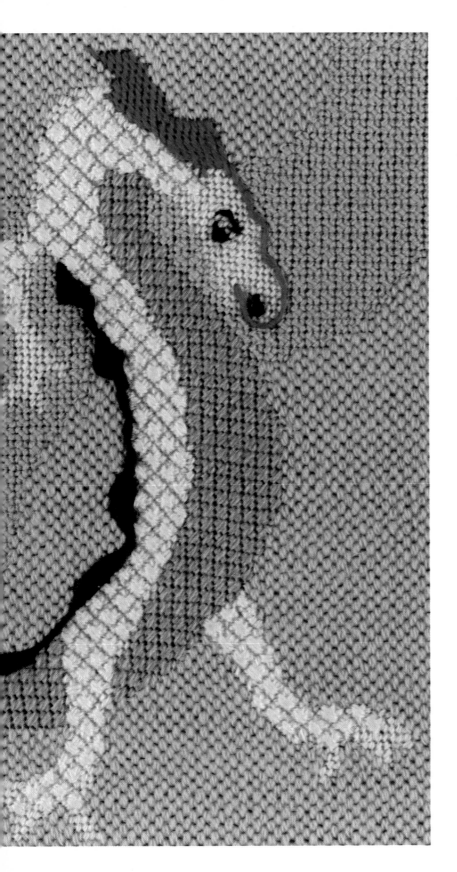

Friendly Dragon. *The most unusual feature of this design is the way that the background has been handled. Two stitches—the rice and the brick—have been used to give additional interest without detracting from the dragon itself. The rice stitch swirl appears darker than the brick stitch portion of the ground. The body is worked in a combination of stitches, which are chosen to look like scales and are tapered into the tent stitch in the areas where the pattern stitches would be too large.*

Blue Flower. *This simple design illustrates how much can be added to very plain needlepoint by giving it a textured background and a few touches of embroidery.*

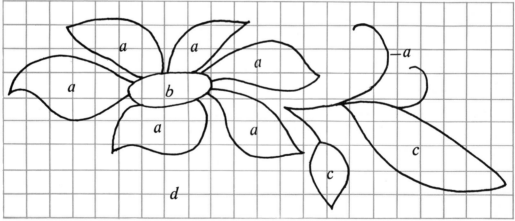

Key to the Stitches

a. *Tent Stitch*
b. *French Knots*
c. *Fishbone Embroidery*
d. *Hungarian Stitch*

Turquoise Flower (detail from larger piece). *The flower itself is worked in the tent stitch and is edged with a whipped running stitch, which has the effect of raising it out of the background. The background of this piece is worked predominately in the mosaic stitch, but several other stitches have been utilized to give the otherwise plain space interest and shadow. If raised stitches are used in this manner, they are very helpful in creating dimension, especially in wall hangings, since reflected light adds to their beauty and creates shadow patterns that otherwise would not be evident.*

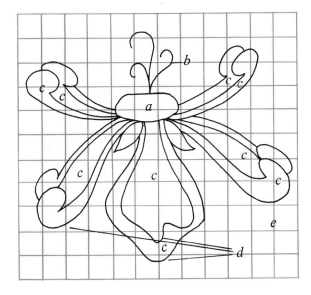

Key to the Stitches

a. *Bullion Knots*
b. *Outline Stitch*
c. *Tent Stitch*
d. *Whipped Running Stitch*
e. *Mosaic Stitch with accents of Scotch, Double Star, Cashmere, Fan, and Double Leviathan Stitch*

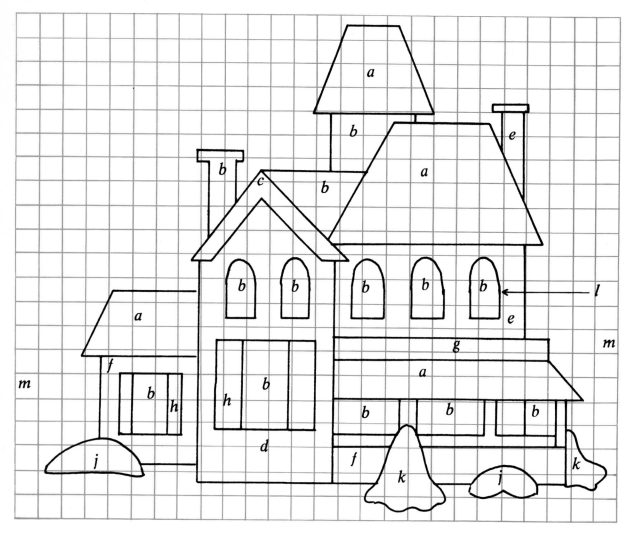

Key to the Stitches

a. *Rice Stitch*
b. *Tent Stitch*
c. *Rope Stitch*
d. *Upright Cross-stitch*
e. *Brick Stitch*
f. *Mosaic Stitch*
g. *Upright Gobelin Stitch*
h. *Slanting Gobelin Stitch*
j. *Buttonhole Stitch*
k. *French Knot on Long Thread*
l. *Couching*
m. *Scotch Stitch*

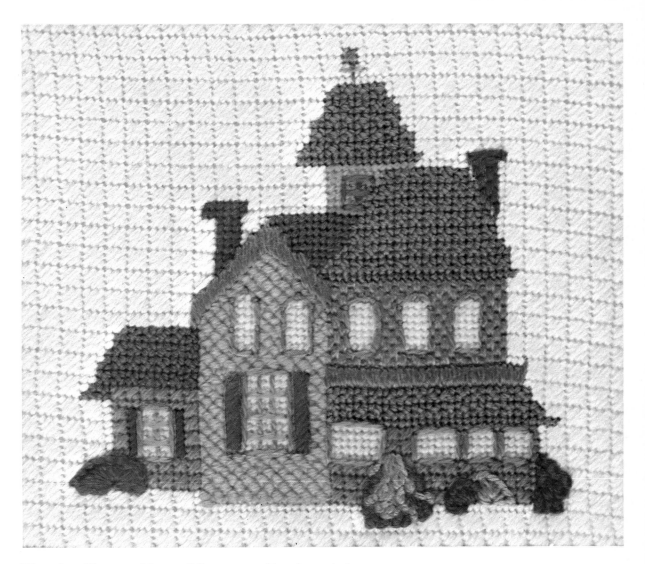

Victorian House. *Many different needlepoint stitches were used in the Victorian house to give it the "gingerbread" look it needed. Small stitches that look like building materials were chosen. Tiny details, such as the weather vane and window outlines, are merely long stitches applied after the rest of the details were finished. The shrubs are buttonhole and French knots on long threads and look much more whimsical than any other stitch could. Combining stitches thus gave the embroiderer much more freedom than if she had attempted to carry out the design in only one stitch.*

Pink Carnation (detail from larger piece). *The pink carnation shows how typical embroidery techniques can be used on needlepoint canvas to shade in a manner impossible with needlepoint stitches. A single strand of crewel wool has been used to work the carnation in straight stitches just as if it were on linen. The needlepoint background was then worked to the edges of the embroidery. Note also the use of whipped spider webs, French knots, and bullion knot details.*

Spring Garden. *Closely massed flowers and bright spring colors work here with a variety of needlepoint stitches to suggest a garden. Small stitches were carefully chosen so that additional pattern would not be added to the already packed design. Since needlepoint stitches have square shapes, all flowers were edged in couching to give them rounded edges and additional dimension. Interesting flower centers are worked in turkey work, French knots, bullion knots, and whipped spider webs.*

Key to the Stitches

a. *Straight Stitch*
b. *Bullion Knots*
c. *Whipped Spider Web*
d. *Diagonal Scotch Stitch*

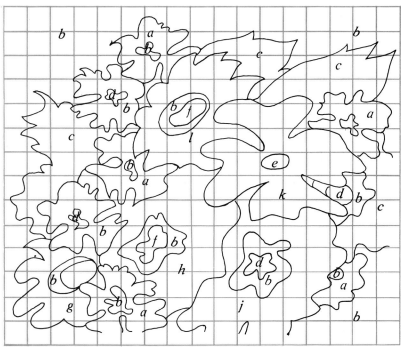

Key to the Stitches

a. *Upright Cross-stitch*
b. *Tent Stitch*
c. *Mosaic Stitch*
d. *French Knots*
e. *Whipped Spider Web*
ƒ. *Turkey Work—cut*
g. *Knotted Stitch*
h. *Smyrna Cross-stitch*
j. *Encroaching Gobelin Stitch*
k. *Double Straight Cross-stitch*
l. *Diagonal Mosaic Stitch*
m. *Bullion Knots*

Key to the Stitches

a. *Outline Stitch*
b. *Satin Stitch*
c. *Turkey Work*
d. *Mosaic Stitch*
e. *Tent Stitch*
f. *Upright Gobelin Stitch*
g. *Straight Stitch*
h. *French Knots*

Little Boy in Red Cap. *Needlepoint and embroidery stitches combine to give this picture its lighthearted quality. The little boy's cap and scarf are worked in outline stitches in rows close to each other to simulate knitting. Since the stitching closely follows the contours of the cap and scarf, they appear more realistic. Unclipped turkey work makes a fluffy pompon on his cap, but it is clipped for the fuzzy little dog. His plaid pants are formed by the mosaic stitch worked in two colors. The Gobelin stitch is used for the grass in the foreground and the fence is long stitches slanting across the canvas to give the effect of rough boards.*

This kind of needlepoint is amusing and quick to do. It is interesting to experiment with stitches to see what effects they can create.

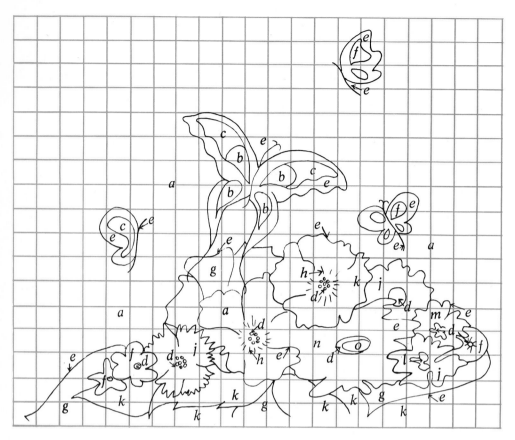

Key to Stitches

a. *Rice Stitch*
b. *Fishbone Stitch*
c. *Tent Stitch*
d. *French Knots*
e. *Couching*
f. *Satin Stitch*
g. *Encroaching Gobelin Stitch*
h. *Straight Stitch*
j. *Long and Short Stitches*
k. *Mosaic Stitch*
l. *Bullion Knots*
m. *Upright Cross Stitch*
n. *Diagonal Mosaic Stitch*
o. *Whipped Spider Web*

Flowers and butterflies. *This very feminine grouping of flowers and butterflies typifies the author's feelings about the combined use of many stitches to create needlepoint embroidery with an individual appearance. Many stitches are used here to emphasize design, but each is carefully chosen to fit the space it fills. When so many textures are part of the design, the background should be as carefully chosen as the stitches. The rice stitch, used here, is gently textured, but small enough not to interfere with the more important design elements.*

8
BARGELLO

Among the best-loved of all types of embroidery throughout history have been the beautiful patterns and colorings of the bargello-type needlepoint. These designs are variously known as Florentine embroidery, flame stitch, and Hungarian point, but they can be collectively designated as bargello. For the most part, these counted repeat designs depend heavily upon color for their particular beauty. Most are worked entirely in the upright Gobelin stitch, but there are several other needlepoint stitches that can be combined with this for variety.

Brown Shadow Boxes. *This type of pattern is most effective if shades of one color are used. The boxes can be enlarged by adding rows to the diamond shape before the lightest rows are worked. If black is the deepest tone used, the depth of the shadow is increased.*

Rose Pattern. *The dark rose row of this pattern establishes the design when the second row is reversed against it. The ensuing design can be filled in any number of ways, each with a different look. This is a popular traditional bargello*

Detail from Gold Chair. *This pattern is a modification of a classic pattern found in many historical pieces of bargello. One beautiful old fragment was worked in silk in shades of blue, yellow, and green. This adaptation uses four shades of gold. To emphasize the lighter tones, the lighter shades were used in greater amounts than the two darker ones. Three rows of the lightest, two of the next shade, and only one each of two deepest ones. The stitches here are also over both two and six threads, creating a most beautiful pattern. Even a difficult-looking pattern like this one is established in the first row, with all succeeding rows merely following it. (See chair on page 35.)*

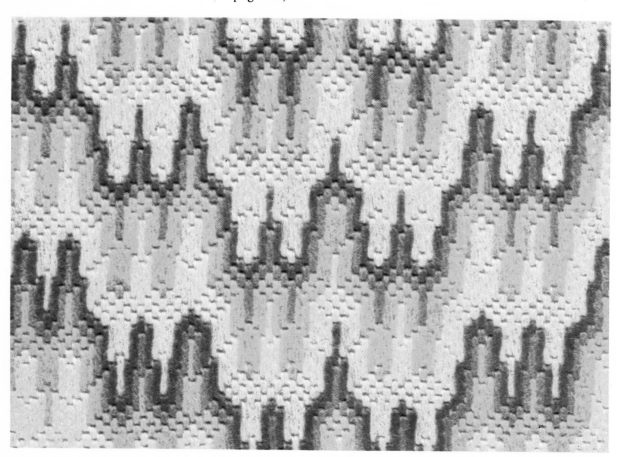

Mitered Bargello Design. *Designs such as this should be called "fun with bargello" for they are fun to work out. The canvas is divided diagonally into quarters (see diagram page 127) and the design worked out. This particular design begins with the outer dark red line. This curved line with two peaks on either side is the basis for the entire design. It is the way in which segments meet at the corners that makes the design interesting. The design could extend to the edges of the piece, but placing it on a tent stitch background emphasizes the motif. This is a great idea for a pillow top.*

Gold Diamonds. *The basic diamond shape here may be done in two manners, both very simple, but the look is great. In one, the center is first worked with a row of upright stitches over four threads, following the outline of the diamond. The remaining center was worked with a diamond eyelet stitch which fits perfectly. The alternate diamond has two rows of upright stitches worked over two threads each. This leaves the same center space to be filled with the diamond eyelet. Just as attractive as this treatment would be a whole piece worked in one of the center manners.*

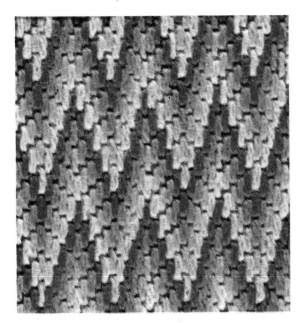 

Lavender Flame. *This is the simplest of the flame patterns, but it is not lacking in beauty because of its simplicity. In fact, simplicity is the charm of the flame pattern. Worked here in four shades of lavender in even peaks of six stitches each, the pattern shows all its assets.*

Green Flame. *Worked in four graduated shades of olive green, this basic flame has been modified by the addition of small peaks alternating with deep ones.*

Pink Wishbone. *Three shades of pink and two lengths of stitches combine to make this design very effective. The dark row is the first one to be worked. The long stitches are six threads long while the shorter ones are only two. Note the way the colors are used in this design. The dark row is the only one with the wishbone shape and appears every fourth row. To accent this, the shades are planned so that this row is always the darkest color. Note also that the two lengths of stitches create an auxiliary pattern in themselves.*

To state that bargello is counted embroidery does not mean that to work it entails many dreary hours of counting. Most of the patterns are simple repeats and follow naturally after the first row is established. The first row must be carefully placed, for a mistake here would mean trouble in every succeeding row.

Generally, bargello is worked on mono canvas, the most popular sizes being number 10 and number 13. However,

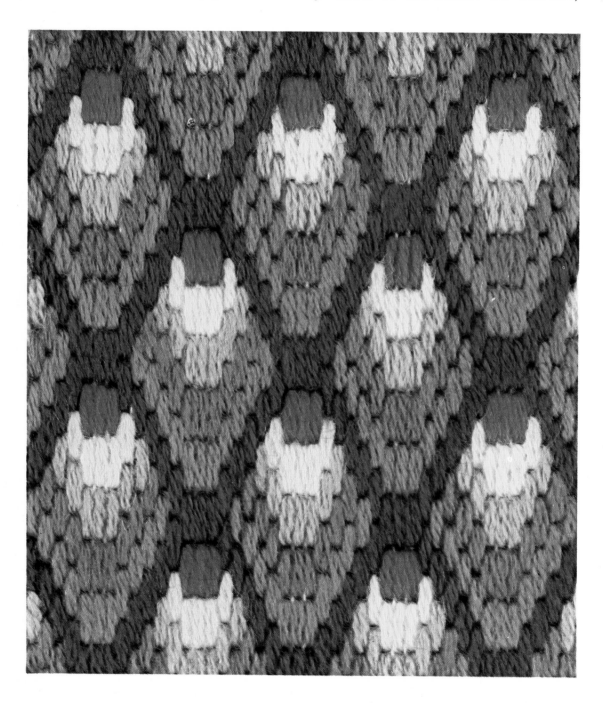

like any other needlepoint, the size can be changed from the very tiniest stitches to the largest, depending upon the effect wished. Traditionally thought of as small stitches beautifully shaded in soft colors, bargello can be surprisingly contemporary worked on large canvas in brilliant colorings.

When bargello is worked on penelope canvas, the pair of vertical threads tends to hold the stitches apart so that the yarn cannot cover the canvas well. This can be overcome by turning the canvas so that the selvedges are at top and bottom (instead of at the sides). The stitches are then placed between the single threads so that they lie close together covering the canvas.

For best appearance, most bargello patterns should be centered on the canvas. To do this, divide the canvas into four equal quarters by drawing one horizontal and one vertical line through the center of the canvas (see drawing). Decide which point of the pattern is the center. Begin working at the center and count the row outward to the left side. End the yarn and go back to the center. Finish the row in the other direction to the right side of the canvas. Stop and carefully check the row. If the pattern is one that is composed of steep peaks, it will be easy to run your finger along the thread that the highest stitches touch to check that all touch the same thread. The first row is usually the key row and any mistake here should be discovered before progressing further.

Succeeding rows can be worked all the way across the canvas either from right to left or vice versa, whichever one is most comfortable. Work the bottom half of the canvas first; then turn the canvas around so that the bottom is now the top and finish this section, being careful to make any adjustments necessary in the sequence of shadings to keep the pattern's continuity.

The upright Gobelin stitch lies vertically on the canvas instead of crossing diagonally as most needlepoint stitches do. Therefore, unless worked with a slightly looser tension than

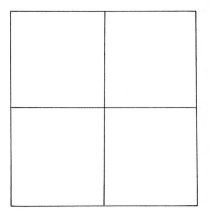

Canvas divided to center Bargello design.

Blue-Shaded Scales. *This is an excellent example of the tricks that color in bargello can play to make a simple design look difficult. The basic pattern is merely a row of diamonds, which have been modified so that, instead of a point, they have three stitches at the top and bottom. The centers are then filled in following the shape of the diamond. It is color that makes the pattern so attractive.*

normal, they will not cover well. If the canvas shows between the stitches, loosen up a little to allow the stitches to "fluff out" and relax.

You will find that, when you work a bargello pattern, the yarn is used up much faster than ordinarily. Use a little bit longer thread—not so long that you have to stretch out your arm full length with each stitch, but long enough to avoid too many ends.

Since the bargello stitches are upright on the canvas, they do not pull the canvas badly out of shape and the piece will probably need very little blocking, or you may find that all the piece really needs is a little freshening. If you are very careful, this can be done with the steam iron. Place a heavy turkish towel over the ironing board surface. Lay the bargello piece face down on the towel. Hold the steam iron over it and let the steam penetrate the yarn. Do not touch the iron to the needlepoint. The long bargello stitches are very easily mashed flat and distorted, ruining the piece. This method of steaming is usually very effective and the result is a new-looking piece of bargello ready for finishing.

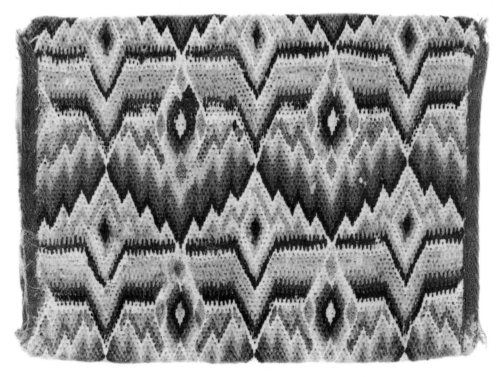

Man's Purse. *This small pocketbook is worked in wool and silk on linen canvas. The stitches are the Florentine and cross. It is dated 1763.*
(Photo courtesy of the Smithsonian Institution)

Bargello Wing Chair. *This beautiful bargello wing chair was made in New England between the years 1720 and 1740. In perfect condition, the bargello covering is worked in lovely, soft shades of blue, rose, tan, yellow, and white wool in an interesting pattern. It is on display in the Williams Room of the Henry Francis du Pont Winterthur Museum.*
(Photo courtesy of the Henry Francis du Pont Winterthur Museum)

THE DEVELOPMENT OF SOME BASIC BARGELLO PATTERNS

An understanding of the way bargello patterns are developed makes it easier to plan and design patterns of your own. Many of the most beautiful patterns begin with the following basic lines or variations of them. All stitches used in the illustration on page 143 are worked over four threads in steps of either one or two. A step is the number of threads up or down that a stitch is worked in relation to the adjacent stitch. For

Man's Purse. *The pocketbook above is flame or Florentine stitches in wool on bast-fiber canvas. Lined in green silk, the purse dates from the eighteenth century. (Detail at left.)* *(Photo courtesy of the Smithsonian Institution)*

instance the flame pattern on the top row is worked in a four-one step with points five stitches high. Each stitch is four threads in height and is placed one thread below the top of the last stitch. This forms the steplike peaks.

Row one

The simplest flame pattern begins with points five stitches high worked in a four-one step. Points can be shorter or longer as desired.

Row two

In this flame pattern, the points are still five stitches in height and the stitches are still four threads long. The compactness of the stitches is caused by working the stitches so that they overlap by two threads instead of one as above. This is called a four-two step.

Row three

This row shows the same basic pattern as the first row, but with the addition of smaller peaks between the tall ones. The variations on this are many since there is no rule about how many different heights can be used in a single pattern.

Row four

This row shows how a curved line is created by increasing gradually the number of stitches in the steps. The shape of the curve is also changed by rearranging the order in which the number of stitches is added.

Row five

This row repeats the second row and adds an identical row of peaks reversed against it. This creates a diamond pattern. If this row had been like the third row, there would be two different-sized diamonds. If the same thing had been done with the fourth row, the result would have been a chain of small medallions.

Experimenting with these basic lines will enable even a beginner to work original patterns. Keep a piece of canvas reserved for these experimental stitchings. You may not come up with the design you need the first time, but it may be something perfectly lovely that you will want to use later. If the original work is on a sampler, it will save much time trying to work it out again.

9
EMBROIDERY STITCHES FOR USE ON CANVAS

In addition to the traditional needlepoint stitches described in the foregoing pages, there are many free or surface embroidery stitches that can be used on needlepoint canvas. These embroidery stitches are usually used as accents or to create a kind of detailing impossible with the needlepoint stitches. A curve, for instance, can be worked first in tent stitch, then outlined and perfected with a line of couching or outline stitches placed on the edge. This technique has been used in some of the needlepoint examples shown in the Design Portfolio; for example, the little boy in the red hat page 127, the butterfly page 116, and the spring flower pictures page 125. These worked needlepoint pictures give many hints on how to use these embroidery stitches in combination with the needlepoint stitches to achieve an effect that would not be possible with only the tent stitch. Note how effectively the flower centers are raised with clusters of French knots, bullion knots, or whipped spider webs. Imagine a little lamb worked entirely in French knots. He would look like he had a coat of curly wool. Once you begin to experiment with the use of the stitches, you will find that your ideas grow and the possibilities are endless.

There is a definite trend toward using needlepoint and embroidery stitches together on needlepoint canvas and since most of the embroidery stitches that are popular are the ones that are currently so widely used as crewel embroidery stitches, the names of the two have been combined by many into the catchy term, crewel point. ("Crewel" is an old Welsh word for wool.) This is a very exciting trend that offers many more possibilities for the creative needlepointer than ever before. The overall effect can be very traditional or completely contemporary, but the textures and dimensions will be entirely of these days. This technique may not be for the purist who believes in using only needlepoint stitches on canvas, but it opens up a whole new vista of experimentation for those willing to adventure. This technique can be expanded until it has been perfected into a fine art, with results that are surprising. Diana Springall's wall hanging, "Summer Garden" (page 151 in Chapter 10), is a striking example of how needlepoint embroidery can be developed to this extent.

Most of the embroidery stitches shown here are familiar to all, but a simple diagram is given to refresh memories if any have been forgotten. Also included is a short discussion showing how each stitch may be used on canvas.

THE CHAIN STITCH

The chain stitch can be worked in rows touching each other to completely cover an area or as an outline stitch to define an area. It is effective either way. The stem of the flower on page 111 has been worked in the chain stitch to give a curved, raised appearance not possible with a flat, square stitch. The pink and orange sections of the bird's tail on page 112 are worked in chain stitches placed right against each other and following the curve of the tail to accent the sweeping line. Detached chain, or lazy daisy, stitches are embroidery accents used in the yellow part of the detail.

THE OUTLINE STITCH

It is possible to use the outline stitch for small thin lines as well as to use rows very close together to cover a whole area. When used close together, the outline stitches can be used very effectively for shading, particularly where a vertical line is desired, as in a tree trunk for instance.

If a solid area is to be filled in with the outline stitch, the stitches are worked on the bare canvas and surrounding stitches, whatever they are, are worked as close as possible. When used for outlining, the stitches can be worked over the other needlepoint stitches.

SATIN STITCH

The satin stitch is worked on canvas exactly as it is on fabric. It can be padded or plain, depending on the depth desired. Work directly on the canvas and work the adjacent stitches as close as possible to the satin stitch edges. Sometimes, when the size of the canvas is large, it is hard to get a neat-looking edge on the satin-stitched area. When this happens, an outline of couching or outline stitches will usually solve the problem, as it did in the little boy's coat on page 127.

FRENCH KNOTS

French knots are very useful accents. A solid cluster will cover a canvas completely or separate knots can be used over other needlepoint stitches where this effect is needed.

It is interesting to use stitches of this type on needlepoint canvas. An acorn looks much more appealing when its cap is a rounded cluster of French knots worked as close to each other as possible. Also, the center of a flower, as suggested in many of the worked needlepoint illustrations in this book, is much more realistic than a flat group of stitches could be. Look at the hair of the little boy in the red cap on page 127. He has blonde French knot curls!

FRENCH KNOT ON A LONG THREAD

Much used for special effects in crewel embroidery, the French knot on a long thread is used the same way on needlepoint canvas. The little pine trees in front of the house on page 123 have been worked in these stitches piled on top of each other and worked in two shades of green to make them even more realistic. This kind of embroidery is fun to do and adds a change to the repetition of stitches that can become tedious.

BUTTONHOLE STITCH

Worked so that the stitches lie close together, the buttonhole stitch will cover the needlepoint canvas well and create interesting variations in texture. Usually, it is most effective when a definite curved outer line is desired. The trees in front of the house on page 123 have been worked in the buttonhole stitch. The trees were placed first. Then the needlepoint stitches of the house were worked so that they fit right up to the edge of the trees without leaving bare canvas threads.

THE BACKSTITCH

Another good outline stitch, the backstitch works out very well on needlepoint canvas. Use much the same way as the chain and outline stitches.

COUCHING

A couching thread can be made to do many tasks that another thread may not be able to accomplish, for the couching may be fastened at strategic points to hold the thread exactly where needed. Couching may also be used effectively to cover whole areas of pattern. This has been done in the yellow section of the bird's tail in the illustration on page 112. The canvas was covered quickly and easily, but an added advantage is that the flowing lines of the tail have been accented by the way the rows of couching threads follow the lines. Tiny details like the outlines of the windows of the house on page 123 can also be carried out well with the maneuverable couching threads.

Sometimes, a heavy or rough type of yarn is needed to create a special texture. But it is almost impossible to thread these kinds of yarn into a needle, much less pull them through the canvas mesh. This is an excellent place to use couching. Any type of thread can be fastened to the canvas with this method. You can see how effectively this can be used in the illustration of Diana Springall's wall hanging on page 151. Use either a thread that matches the yarn exactly or a contrast for the fastening thread.

BULLION KNOTS

The coils of bullion knots are very interesting accents and, used in a cluster, will cover the canvas. However, they are not practical for anything except detail work. They make good flower centers and can also be used to form small flowers and similar small details.

THE WHIPPED SPIDER WEB

The whipped spider web will be a raised detail on the top of the canvas and will, therefore, be a very showy addition to a piece of needlepoint. The individual motifs are good as flower centers or to suggest small flowers. Many different effects can be achieved with this stitch just as when it is used in crewel embroidery.

THE STRAIGHT STITCH

The straight stitch is handled on canvas in the same manner as it is on the more traditional linen fabric. It is very useful for shading and creating textural interest. By using the straight stitch on the head and body of the bird on page 112 it was possible to shade the colors from pale yellow into the dark aqua without a break in the flow of color. Straight stitches also create a more textured background for the little boy on page 127. The fence is worked in straight stitches placed diagonally to form rough-looking boards. Used in random lengths, but placed in even horizontal rows, straight stitches suggest the sky above the fence.

The straight stitch can also be used as it is in crewel embroidery for delicately shaded flowers and leaves. It is even attractive to work the straight stitches in a finer wool, giving much more latitude as far as shading is concerned. A floral bouquet, for instance, can be worked as if it were on linen, with a needlepoint background worked around it. This combination of the two embroidery techniques is most interesting and effective.

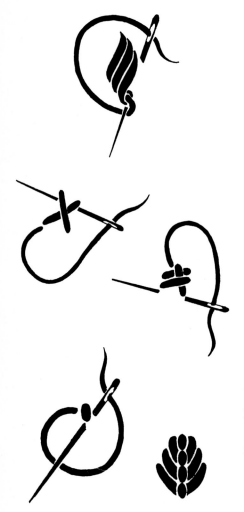

THE ROPE STITCH

The rope stitch produces a braidlike, raised line which can be worked to be either wide or narrow. It may be used in closely spaced rows to completely cover an area, but it is usually more effective as a line stitch. The slanting roof line of the house on page 123 shows the rope stitch used to good advantage. A flower stem is another way of using the rope stitch to maximum advantage.

THE CLOSE HERRINGBONE STITCH

Worked with all stitches of equal length, the close herringbone stitch will be a neat, fat braid. If desired, the stitches can taper to a point and the stitch will work out as a leaf stitch. Use this stitch in the same manner and for the same purposes as it is used in crewel embroidery.

THE FISHBONE STITCH

Used for a leaf stitch, the fishbone makes a very attractive realistic-looking leaf, complete down to the center vein. This stitch covers the canvas well and combines well with many needlepoint stitches, which can be worked right up to the edge of the fishbone.

This is by no means the complete list of embroidery stitches that can be used on needlepoint canvas. Rather, it is a sampling to interest the reader in trying this technique of canvas embroidery and exploring its delights.

To those who feel that this kind of embroidery is not needlepoint, there is one reply. Simply defined, needlepoint is embroidery over the threads of a canvas. As soon as embroidery is placed on the canvas, it becomes needlepoint. But no matter what the definition, this is the direction in which needlepoint is going, and it is good. It is fun and challenging. The truly creative needleworker is seeking a freer expression in needlework than has ever before been found and crewel point seems to be the answer.

Once your needlepoint is completed, with or without the embroidery stitches, a very happy ending for it is the addition of your initials and the date. This will make the needlepoint very personally yours and add to both your own and you family's enjoyment of it. For this purpose a little alphabet and numerals are included below for you to stitch as desired.

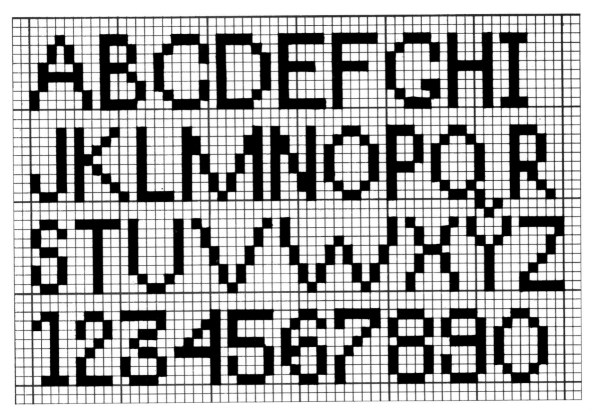

10 BLOCKING, FINISHING, AND MOUNTING

There is a great deal of difference in the much desired "hand-made" look and the sloppy "homemade" look so often seen. This is really a shame because in most cases as much work went into the less professional-looking item as into its attractive counterpart. The difference is often the blocking—or lack of it.

BLOCKING

Even if you have been able to keep your piece clean and straight while working, it still needs blocking to give it the crisp, new look you want. If you are like most needlepointers, the piece is wrinkled and crushed and very much out of shape.

Blocking will not remove mistakes. It will, however, make the stitches look evener and smoother. Above all, it will restore the canvas to its original condition and correct any stretching that occurred during the working.

The size of a needlepoint piece cannot be changed by blocking it larger or smaller. For this reason, measuring and planning at the beginning of a project are very important.

The blocking process is a relatively simple one, but one that must be carried out with precision. It is also something that every needlepointer should try at least once, for the experience provides a knowledge of the kind of labor involved and an insight that will be valuable if you later decide to have your needlepoint professionally blocked.

You will need a blocking board and a supply of rustproof nails or tacks. The tacks can be either aluminum or copper. An old drawing board makes a good blocking board, but a piece of fiberboard or plywood will do nicely. The board must have a smooth surface that you do not mind marring with nail holes and be of a type that the wet needlepoint will not cause to warp.

Although not generally used for needlepoint, one of the finest blocking boards is a doily blocker which is available in the needlework department in most stores. It is a square of pressed hardboard marked both horizontally and vertically with lines spaced one inch apart. There are perforations along these lines into which the nails are inserted. A good supply of aluminum nails comes with the board. The invest-

Summer Garden. *Colors and qualities suggesting a country garden are used here for an abstract wall hanging. A variety of different textured yarns, as well as different stitches contribute to the charming effect.*
(Panel by Diana Springall, photo courtesy of B.T. Batsford Ltd.)

ment in a doily blocker is very small, but its contribution to easy blocking is great. If you plan to do a lot of needlepoint, try to find one and use it.

The outline of the finished needlepoint should be drawn either on the board or on a piece of paper taped to it. The center of each side should be indicated. These will be the first points to be fastened.

Carefully remove the masking tape from the edges of the needlepoint so that you do not take too many canvas threads with it. Turn under the raw edges of the canvas and stitch firmly. If for any reason you do not have a two-inch border of unworked canvas on all sides, you will have to extend the edges by attaching an extension of firm, colorfast fabric. Stitch a double thickness of the fabric to the canvas and make the extension wide enough so that you do not have to put tacks into the worked needlepoint itself.

Find and mark the center of each side of the canvas. Do this by actually counting the mesh. Mark with a thread or waterproof marker.

To be blocked, the needlepoint must be dampened. To insure that both the canvas and the yarn are completely and evenly damp, roll the piece in a thoroughly moistened towel and leave it overnight. The towel should be very wet but not dripping and of course only cold water is to be used.

When the needlepoint is removed from the towel, it will be very limp. The sizing in the canvas is wet and the needlepoint is pliable and more amenable to the stretching. When dry the sizing will return to its original crispness.

Pulling the canvas as tightly as possible, tack the marked centers of the sides of the canvas to the center marks on the blocking board. Working outward from these points, tack the canvas at one-inch intervals along the edges until you have tacked all four sides completely. This is usually easiest to do if you tack a few points on one side, turn the board, place a few tacks opposite those tacks, and continue until the canvas is fastened. If the canvas is stubborn, do not be afraid to pull. The canvas was strong to begin with and you have added the strength of the yarn.

In many cases, especially in pieces worked in the continental stitch, one corner is very crooked. It may be necessary to move the tacks several times before you are able to work the piece into a straight position on the board. The canvas will stay wet and pliable long enough for you to tack and retack, if necessary.

Sometimes a needlepoint piece is very much out of shape. This is usually the result of the stitches having been worked too tightly. In these cases it seems that the canvas will never be straight. If this happens, tack the piece into place as nearly straight as possible and leave to dry. Redampen and repeat the blocking process. The second time is not nearly as much trouble as the first and is definitely worthwhile. Some badly misshapen pieces may need to be blocked two or three times.

The needlepoint must stay on the blocking board until it is completely dry. The board should lie flat and should never be placed near heat or in direct sunlight. The time needed for drying will, of course, vary with the weather conditions. Don't try to shorten the drying time by removing the needlepoint from the board while wet. The canvas will return to its unblocked shape.

Keep in mind that blocking is the only method for straightening needlepoint. You cannot correct a crooked piece by sewing or mounting. A pillow that starts out as a misshapen piece of needlepoint will always have an odd shape.

Needlepoint cannot be successfully blocked with the steam iron. The canvas must dry in the straightened position and there is no practical way to accomplish this with the steam iron. Never press your needlepoint with the iron. The stitches will be mashed flat and distorted. There may, however, be times when the needlepoint needs only a little freshening. This can be done by holding the iron above the needlepoint and allowing the steam to penetrate the yarn. The iron should never be allowed to rest on the needlepoint.

FINISHING AND MOUNTING

It is not the purpose of this book to go into the exact sewing and mounting techniques in detail. There are a few general rules that will interest most readers.

Some projects are easily finished at home with only a little basic knowledge of sewing and construction. These are the smaller, easy to handle items, such as pillows, belts, pin cushions, tote bags, eyeglass cases, slip seats, book covers, bookends, and doorstops. It is safe to assume that if the project is one that you would attempt to make from a fine fabric, you will be successful in making it from your needlepoint. Basically, needlepoint is a fine quality, but heavy fabric, and should be handled as such.

Large upholstered furniture is naturally finished more successfully by a professional. If the cost of this service seems high, consider that the needlepoint's excellent wearing qualities will probably make it unnecessary to ever have the piece covered again. A set of chairs in the Bargello Museum in Florence dates back to the seventeenth century. What greater economy could there be than in an investment like that!

Needlepoint purses are very elegant fashion accessories and another case in which the skill of the professional is desired. In addition to his expertise in finishing the needlepoint, he will have an array of handles, frames, and leather dyed in the latest fashion colors. These are the things that will make you proud to carry your needlepoint bag. Properly cared for, a needlepoint bag will give years of service and pleasure. Be sure to keep this in mind when choosing the design for a bag and make your choice one that will be fashionable for a long time.

While discussing needlepoint bags, it might be a good idea to remind the reader that the same people who make up your bag also have a repair service. There may be a lovely petit point bag stored somewhere in your house because it is soiled or damaged in some way. If the needlepoint is still good, consider having it remounted. Most department stores have this service and you may be surprised at how lovely Grandmother's old evening bag can be.

Removable slip seats on chairs can be easily replaced by anyone. There is only one trick to this—pull the needlepoint very tightly and tack firmly. Remove old upholstery and replace padding if necessary. Position needlepoint on the seat, centering the design. Tack in place. Pull needlepoint at corners and make a series of small pleats to take up the extra fullness. Cover the bottom of the seat with muslin to cover raw edges of the needlepoint and the profusion of tacks.

Book covers are merely rectangles of needlepoint with pockets on either end into which the cover of the book is inserted. Measure carefully when planning a book cover to allow enough width to allow the book to close. Do this by inserting the tape measure into the book just inside the front cover, closing the book, and measuring all the way to the edge of the back cover. It is a good idea to allow an extra one-quarter inch on all sides so that the book will fit into the finished cover.

With the advent of the new iron-on interfacings, putting together a fashion belt becomes very simple. Trim away excess canvas to one-half inch on all sides. Press the edges to the inside with steam iron. Cut the iron-on interfacing to the shape of the belt, but make it one-eighth inch smaller on all sides. Bond it to the belt following the instructions that come with the interfacing. Cover the facing with ribbon slip-stitched to the edge of the belt. Attach a buckle. Take the belt to the shoemaker and ask him to insert eyelets. He has a heavy type that is more suitable to the thick needlepoint than those available to the home sewer.

These methods are applicable primarily for a fashion accessory belt intended for only a few seasons' wear. If a classic belt is desired, it should be finished by being mounted on leather by the same craftsman who mounts needlepoint bags.

Needlepoint pillows can be made up in as many ways as decorative fabric pillows. Your personal preference is the guide to this as well as to the choice of fabric for the backing. The fabric should be of good quality to do justice to the needlepoint. Color can either match the background or pick up one of the colors in the design.

A spray of soil retardant is a good way to finish any needlepoint project. It will not affect the colors and will provide a measure of protection for the many hours that went into the project. Use on pictures and wall hangings as well as on items that will be handled and more easily soiled.

There will always be a debate about whether or not glass should be used over a needlepoint picture. Naturally, the stitching of the needlepoint will be more beautifully displayed without the glass. There are, however, areas in the country where, because of atmospheric conditions this is just simply not practical. If you live in one of these large metropolitan areas, by all means have glass installed in the frame. Do use the new etched glass that is glare-proof for the best results.

Naturally, the amount of finishing and mounting that you undertake is going to be limited by both your ability and your feelings about your needlepoint. The price of having a pillow finished, for example, is very high when the little time to make it is considered. But you may have an especially lovely piece of needlepoint into which enough labor has already been invested to make the cost of having it professionally finished worthwhile. It may be for a gift that you want to be extra special. All these things are to be considered before making the decision to do it yourself. There is a great deal of satisfaction in doing the entire project yourself that leads most of us down this path.

INDEX